Ian Nicolson's Guide To Boat Buying

By the same author:

Sea Saint

Log of the Maken

Building the St Mary

Dinghy Cruising

Outboard Boats and Engines

Ian Nicolson's Guide to Boat Buying

Adlard Coles Ltd   London

Published 1969 in Great Britain by Adlard Coles Ltd.
3 Upper James Street, Golden Square, London W1

Printed in Great Britain
by Ebenezer Baylis & Son Ltd.
The Trinity Press, Worcester, and London

SBN: 229 97468 6

Dedicated to S. M. B. Hardwicke

Contents

Plates

Introduction
What it is all about

There was once a yachtsman who was typical of the breed. He loved yachts dearly and spent the greater part of his life sailing, talking about boats, planning new ones, buying bits and pieces to go on his current yacht and dreaming about his loves. After many years of this, his wife extracted a promise from him that he would build no more yachts. To this he agreed, but not long afterwards, his boat was wrecked when her mooring failed in a gale. The yachtsman walked along the shore till he came across the scattered woodwork, which was the total remains of his craft. The biggest piece of wreckage was the fore-hatch top, a piece of wood about 2 ft square and an inch thick.

He picked up this forehatch and with it walked to Fife's famous yacht yard. He sought out Willy Fife and handed him the fore-hatch and said:

'Just repair my yacht, will you?'

This is how the *Ayrshire Maid* came to be built, seventy years ago. She is shown in plate eleven of this book, because she is symbolic of that determination which grips all boat-owners. Once a man, woman or child has owned a yacht, that person is never again free from the overpowering wish to have a boat.

This wish, which amounts to a contagious disease, has odd effects. People reject good jobs in order to be able to live near their favourite sailing centre. Others keep well-paid jobs but fly or motor vast distances each weekend to get afloat. Some pawn family heirlooms to buy boats, others work far into the night to earn enough to buy a boat. Still others are hard at it till the early hours of the morning, building their own boat in kitchen, garage or garden. This urge to have a boat is a disease, but it is the healthiest disease that ever existed!

It gives a vast number of people life-long enjoyment, as there is no need to stop through old age. There is no reason for waiting awhile before starting either. Each of my own children has started racing in the first few months of their lives. It adds extra excitement to our races when my wife calls up from the cabin:

'Don't tack for a moment, till I've emptied the baby's bath-water.'

The sheer excitement, pleasure and diverse enjoyment of owning a boat is full justification for any sacrifices that have to be made to get one. Also, it is worth remembering that the majority of boats will last fifty years and more, and so they represent remarkably good investments.

This book is a guide for anyone who wants to buy a boat, or improve his existing boat. It is written with the knowledge that boat-buying is an art. This means that there are many aspects that are matters of personal opinion, if not prejudice. As a result, some yachtsmen will not agree with everything I write. This is hardly surprising, since it is a basic principle of yachting that no three yachtsmen ever agree on any two subjects. But then, half the pleasure of reading any book is finding passages to contradict. The other half of the pleasure is finding paragraphs which confirm your own prejudices.

Prices are steadily being inflated and therefore readers should take note that prices mentioned may even now err on the low side.

1   *The time to buy*

Yachting in Britain, and indeed in most countries, is very much affected by the seasons. Many owners want their boats afloat by Easter, and everyone, just everyone, makes sure they are afloat by Whitsun.

As it takes several weeks to fit out even a small boat, the result of this 'afloat-by-Easter' flap is that all the yards are extremely busy during the spring. This is the time when second-hand prices are highest. Owners who have not sold over the winter tend to change their minds, and decide to hold on to their boats for another season. Of course if an owner has bought another boat, or is moving away from the district, or has some other reason which makes a sale imperative, then he may be more inclined to lower his price, even in the spring. But there will be buyers about, brokers are busy and optimistic, the sun shines, yachting magazines work up everyone's enthusiasm for the coming months' excitement afloat, and all in all, there are few owners who are going to be persuaded to make much of a reduction in price in March.

By May things have changed. An owner who has not sold suddenly realises that most people are afloat. He is faced with the prospect of paying another year's laying up bills, another year's laid-up insurance. He sees his capital tied up uselessly, his boat one year older. If she lies all summer in a shed her topsides' seams will open if she is wood-planked, dust accumulates, she gets more bedraggled. He starts to drop his price. By July most owners are resigned to holding their boats until the autumn selling season. In practice quite a few boats do change hands in this month, especially if the weather has been good. If the Stock Market booms, this helps too, in my opinion.

September is the month in which to buy. Now owners are thinking of having new boats built. They

The time to buy look back over the season and consider that the only reason they did not win the Points Cup was that they had an outdated yacht. Owners are faced with the cost of hauling the boat up, and if they can sell while the boat is still afloat that means a useful saving.

If a boat is bought in September, she can be given a trial sail before she is hauled up. The survey can be postponed till the boat is ashore, but once she is hauled up the new owner has the whole winter to make changes in rig, accommodation, deck gear and so on. If the ship has to be sailed a long way to her new home port, then September is not too late in the year for reasonably comfortable cruising (though I must admit I used to have some of my best cruises in November).

Plenty of boats change hands in October, but by the end of that month things quieten down a lot. Buyers mutter: 'I'll wait to see what there is at the Boat Show,' even though they know that they do not intend to get a new yacht. Normally December is a quiet month for brokers, but there are usually a few far-seeing buyers who have not found anything in the autumn, and are determined not to be caught by the hardening prices of the spring.

During the early part of January all the world, his wife and children are either just going, or just coming or are at the London Boat Show. The whole second-hand market wakes up, and purchases increase in frequency, up to the spring pinnacle again.

Some years the pattern changes to a certain degree. A stinging budget, a prolonged spell of good weather, sometimes, though to a lesser extent a bout of bitter weather, credit squeezes, are typical disrupting factors. But combined they do not much change the basic pattern.

The Snapdragon 26 is one of the few small cruisers which sleeps five. Intended particularly for estuary cruising, she has twin fin keels so that she sits upright when aground. There is an outboard well aft, which makes a very good stowage place for a deflated rubber dinghy if an inboard engine is fitted. The builders are Thames Marine of Charfleet, Canvey, Essex.

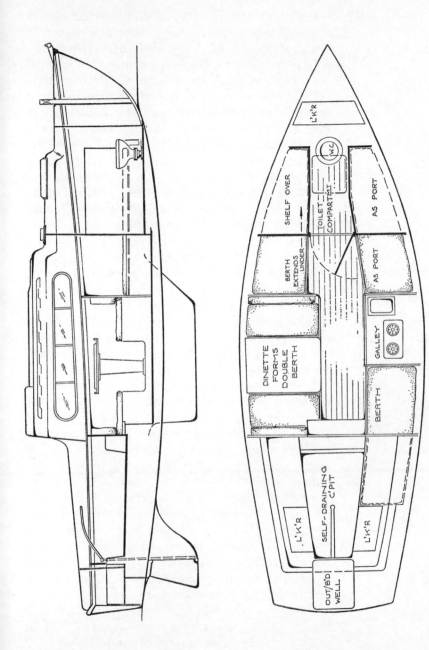

Ordering a new boat presents an entirely different set of problems. A yacht between 5 and 90 tons takes about 5 to 7 months to build. Anyone who tries to build faster only finds that there is not room round the hull and inside it to get more men onto the job. Of course there are plenty of exceptions to this rule. A fibreglass yacht, built from an existing mould can often be built in one to three months, and for a 5 tonner this could be cut to 1 week when the joinery is mass-produced so that there are patterns for each part. This assumes that the boat is built as one of a series production. If it is in any way special, then the delay of one item, such as the transducer for the echo-sounder, can hold up the launching of the whole boat. Just one little item. That is why yachts are so often delivered late.

Taking the 6 months building period as a basis, it would seem at first sight that for a boat wanted in April, the order can be safely placed in the first week of November. This is quite wrong, because building time and designing time must be separated. For a one-design, or restricted class of cruiser, or some boat already designed, there is little delay between placing the order with the builder and starting work. But if the design has to be started from the first clean sheet of paper, then an extra fortnight as an absolute minimum must be allowed. And that assumes the boat in question is a simple yacht, say a conventional 6 tonner. For a boat that requires a lot of planning, it is not too much to allow 6 weeks between the day the designer starts work and the day the loftsman begins laying the lines down.

For highly competitive boats, it is essential to allow far longer. Time must also be found in the design office to start on the job. It is too much to expect everyone in the design office to drop everything just to start work on one particular special yacht. If there is to be tank testing, then not only does this take time, but there are further days expended making the models.

However a factor which is just as important as designing and building times, is the availability of yards. If the order for a new boat is deferred until November, it will be found that most of the good yards have no berths left. For series-produced boats things are different, because at the end of the summer and autumn the firms may well be building up stocks, and a November order may be in good time for delivery in the early spring. But a special boat, built in the traditional, or mainly traditional way should be ordered as early in the summer as possible. This gives the designer a chance to tackle the job with plenty of thinking time. It means that the builder can get all the parts and material ordered in ample time. Most important of all, the yard can start building when times are slack, as they always are once the fitting-out season is over at the end of May.

The ideal way to go about things is to decide just a year ahead, unless the boat is really special, something like a class II ocean-racer aimed at the Admirals Cup. In that case a year is hardly enough. Go to the chosen designer right away, and give him the outline of the required boat. He can start to clear his mind and his drawing board, he can have a quiet chat with the managers of the best yards, and tentatively reserve berths. Selected logs can be examined and set aside, engine-makers can be asked about their plans in case a rather special power unit with a particularly favourable power-weight ratio is about to be offered for sale.

So far the whole discussion has been on which month to choose for buying a second-hand boat, or ordering a new one. There is one rather important point about timing, which applies to both new and second-hand boats.

The purchase of anything so special as a boat is not to be scrambled, hurried, or otherwise carried out without much pondering, weighing of pros and cons.

This sort of decision cannot happily be made on a Saturday morning, or on a Sunday. Designers find all their clients arrive around coffee time on Saturday, and there is not sufficient time available for the true serious business of planning a boat. Yard managers are harassed by owners making complaints, asking to be launched three weeks earlier, or merely the whereabouts of the fresh-water tap. In this hubbub it is impossible to get a manager to concentrate on what matters to you, the momentous purchase of a yacht.

So take a mid-week day off work, invent a grandmother due for interment, or have a fictitious toothache. If the Managing Director, foreman, senior partner or whoever it is that commands your destiny is human, tell him you need a whole day off to buy a boat. If he refuses, change your job. It is no good working under a man who has his values all mixed up.

2 *The search*

One autumn I spent a lot of time pottering along the south coast in a beamy little dinghy. She was a 10-footer, I recall, and handy as a scooter. I could, and did, work into any creek small enough to be called a drain, and could haul her up the beach single-handed. It was a grand way to get from yard to yard, and I had the chance to see a lot of boats at very little expense. In fact this is in some ways the ideal method of going in search of a boat, though I realise now that I should have taken rather more precautions than I did. A small dinghy is not really suitable transport after dark, just before Christmas, outside estuaries. But a dinghy can be a great boat for limited coastal cruising, provided it is sensibly used.†

Many boatyards are down long muddy lanes, so that they are not easy to find, nor is the approach kind to cars. But by sailing along the coast, from yard to yard, one gets additional pleasure from the search. A dinghy may not be suitable, and an alternative is to charter a boat. This gives you a chance to learn about one more yacht (the one you are chartering) and perhaps a bit more about the waters you will be using once you have found your dream-ship. It is cheap transport, and you have somewhere to stay each night, whereas if you go by car you have the daily problem of finding a hotel. Particularly very early and very late in the season charter rates are at their lowest. In some cases boats are available at less than half the mid-summer charges, if hired in March, April, September and October. At this time of year too, it is possible to charter for weekends only.

Before visiting a yard it is important to telephone or write giving the day and time you will arrive. This is because some yards close for all or part of the weekend.

† See *Dinghy Cruising*, by Ian Nicolson, published by Adlard Coles Ltd.

Many close at 4.30 p.m. on weekdays, and anyway, it is inconvenient to arrive just when the yard manager is dealing with another visitor.

The important thing, when writing, is to say which boat you want to see, so that the yard can have the cover taken off the boat, and a wandering lead light laid on. At the same time, mention that you are interested in other boats of the same general type, in case there are any for sale in the yard. It must be admitted that quite a few yards will not strip the tarpaulin off a boat, nor have the lighting ready till the prospective buyer arrives. This is because they have been let down so many times.

Those boat show-rooms and chandlers which have almost all come into existence within the last ten years, and which usually specialise in yachts under 25 feet, are normally open all day Saturday. Some open Sunday too. But Saturday is the one day when everyone goes to them. As buying a boat is for most people a momentous step, not to be rushed, it is worth taking some trouble to avoid completing the purchase on a Saturday, when the salesmen are over-busy, and cannot give their best attention. It is probably best to make a careful inspection of the boat in the showroom first, and for this the salesman is not needed. This part of the job can be done on a Saturday, but even then there will be the distraction of so many other people crowding round. Unless of course one goes in the autumn or winter, when the showroom will probably be deserted.

These showrooms are run much as motor-car selling establishments, and many are offshoots of the car industry. They advertise in the local and yachting press. One of their major assets is that they will take second-hand boats in part exchange. This is at present a service which virtually no other part of the yachting industry offers.

While the showroom is a usual place to start looking for a *new small* boat, a second-hand boat is normally found through a broker, or through a classified advertisement in the yachting press. There are also some local newspapers, such as the *Southern Daily Echo* and the

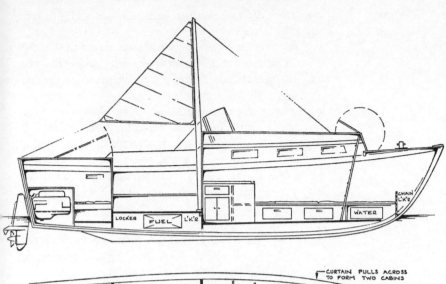

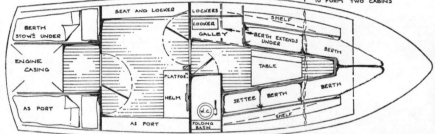

This design of a six-berth motor cruiser is by A. Mylne and Co. of 6 Royal Terrace, Glasgow. Though the speed is moderately fast steadying sails are carried. These add greatly to the comfort aboard when fishing, or lazing along at half throttle. In an overall length of 33′ 6″ there is more privacy than usual, with a double cabin aft, separate toilet, and divideable main cabin.

Glasgow Herald which have regular columns of classified advertisements for boats.

Yachting magazines vary in that some have long columns of classified ads, others hardly any. All have advertisements put in by brokers, and this is a handy way to get hold of the addresses of brokers. Another way to get addresses of brokers is to write to the Yacht Brokers, Designers and Surveyors Association, at

Orchard Hill, The Avenue, Farnham Lane, Haslemere, Surrey.

A few brokers specialise, but most cover the whole field of yachts for sale except the very large and the smallest such as racing dinghies. As the profit on the sale of a second-hand dinghy is so small and office costs so high, few brokers handle the sale of dinghies and similar very small boats. Such boats are either bought through classified ads or through a showroom or chandler, or by making inquiries at yacht clubs. Some clubs have notice-boards set aside for the particulars of boats for sale. This is often the best place to find a class racing yacht.

It is natural that brokers' advertisements cannot list every boat available. The broker will tend to detail the 'plums' he has to offer. When writing to a broker, or calling at his office it is usual to ask for particulars of whatever advertised boat takes your fancy. The broker will almost always offer similar boats as well. Also he knows from experience that plenty of buyers say that they are interested in a 6-ton sloop but settle finally for a 10-ton yawl. For this reason brokers tend to send details of boats roughly approximating to the buyer's requirements. They tend to offer boats bigger and smaller, with different engines, rigs and accommodations to what has been asked for.

Some buyers get annoyed by this 'spread', but there is a second good reason why brokers do not stick exactly to the buyer's specification. Often the buyer wants a type or size of boat which is not available, or not for sale in the broker's area, or not available at the buyer's price. Also the broker knows that it often does not cost so very much to change the accommodation, the rig or the engine. For instance a 25-ton sloop, which a small family could never handle safely can sometimes be turned into a snug ketch for about £600 or maybe £750. Because the 25-tonner is too big for most owners when sloop-rigged, it is likely to be on the market at a lower price than the same size of boat ketch-rigged. (This assumes that both boats are otherwise equal, and that the rigs are both modern, of their type.) It is there-fore sometimes more sensible to buy the cheaper sloop and convert, since in the long run this may cost less. Even if it costs slightly more it means that the finished conversion will have new gear and some new sails, and for that reason some items will not need fitting out. So again this would be the cheapest long-term course.

All these factors the broker automatically balances in his mind, and this explains why so many prospective buyers get details of boats which do not seem to suit them at all. Where brokers *are* lax is that they do not write and explain these factors to prospective buyers.

When writing to a broker, or calling, the first thing to tell him is your top price limit. He also wants to know your favoured size limits, and what you intend to do with the boat. Your usual crew might be mentioned, if it consists of people who are less than total assets. Triplets under four do not make up in numbers what they lack in experience and muscle. It is not enough to say you want a 'family' sailing yacht because to some people this means an ocean racer which only falls short of being an out-and-out racing machine by virtue of its moderately powerful diesel engine. To others a family sailing cruiser is a twin screw motor-yacht (with three toilets, a bath and a shower) which has steadying sails that are set only in fine weather.

Some brokers take their clients round to view boats. They do this when they are not busy, or if they consider the client worth the time expended. A buyer who is new to yachting, or new to the kind of sailing he plans, is well advised to try and lure the broker to come round viewing with him. This way the full value of the broker's years of experience are gained. But it is not much use turning up at short notice on a Saturday morning in March and expecting the broker to drop everything just to join in a jolly little jaunt to view a couple of three tonners.

It is no secret that brokers do not have a life of cream buns and twenty-hour working weeks. In fact they have to put in long hours. Just when every right-thinking mortal is going off sailing, at the weekends, the brokers have to work hardest. Their profits are eaten into by the cost of advertising, which is a very essential part of their job. To give an indication of the amount of their clerical work, I know one broker who did a bit of research and found out that for every boat he sold, he dictated, and his secretary typed, 250 letters.

This is not a tearful defence of brokers, who after all have presumably chosen this method of earning their livelihood. But it does give a few pointers as to how to get the best out of their professional services.

Some brokers make a special point of offering only boats they know themselves. This is the type of man who will save you a vast amount of time. Above all he will save those maddening journeys to the far end of the sixth county away, to view some proposed bargain which turns out to be a complete dud. This point is so important that it is worth while, before going on any long or inconvenient trip to view a boat, to ask the broker if he knows the owner or the boat. If he honestly recommends the boat, ask him when he last went aboard because a good boat can go far down-hill in three years of neglect.

Many broking firms are linked with designers and surveyors, and often a single company does all three jobs. One partner or member of the firm will probably specialise in each side of the firm's work. Here the best firms will have a constant interchange of information between the various branches. What occasionally happens though, is that one man is so busy that he seldom has time to talk to his partners, the chief draughtsman, the senior surveyor, and so on. In this sort of instance the very busy firm may not be the one that gives you the best all-round service, from the brokerage point of view.

There are a few brokers who refuse to handle survey work at all. They feel that the two jobs are mutually antagonistic. This argument rather weakens when it is realised how important it is for every broker to know as much as possible about the boats he is selling. A succession of surveys done by an office keeps that firm right up to the mark. The survey of one yacht of a class indicates what her sister ships are likely to suffer from. Boats of a class deteriorate in the same places and react in the same ways to modernising, or hard driving, and have parallel rates of depreciation.

Looking for a definite type of boat, it sometimes pays to concentrate, at least initially, on a given area because certain types tend to congregate in particular regions. For instance Essex is very much the home of shoal draft sailing cruisers under 10 tons, and the Solent has a good collection of fast offshore power yachts, because racing for this type is mainly centred thereabouts.

One final precept which I think is rather important. Before settling for a particular yacht, it is worth looking at about forty. This is not to say that the first one examined is not the right one. It is just that without seeing forty it is hard to be sure that the market has been fully investigated. But if, after viewing more than forty boats the dream-ship of your waking hours has not been found, then either:

1. She does not exist, or
2. You have not got enough money for her, and must reduce your ideas, or settle down and earn, win or borrow more money, or
3. You are looking for something rather special and will have to build or convert to get what you want, or
4. You have searched with energy but without sense, and are looking in the wrong places.

This 'forty-boat' rule is most useful. If you think that you have the right boat, but are unsure, apply the rule. If you have only viewed ten boats, go on looking, and if necessary come back to your original choice. One time when you cannot afford to apply the rule is in the late spring, when you must make a decision, often enough, without delay. Otherwise you will either not get afloat that season, or someone else will buy the boat you favour while you are examining the rest of the market.

3   *Boat shows*

On the first Wednesday in January each year, the London Boat Show opens at Earls Court. It lasts for ten days, starts at 10 am, closes at 9 pm and is open daily except Sundays.

Those are the bare facts which cover one of the great yachting events of the year. Indeed it is very hard not to wax excessively enthusiastic about the London Boat Show, because it is so good, so successful, so far ahead of some other Shows, and it gives a buyer such a fabulous opportunity to view, compare, price, discuss and cogitate.

The Show is so big that it cannot be seen in one day. In fact anyone interested in the yachting industry, and that means virtually all enthusiastic yachtsmen, can spend five days in the Show and still be finding interesting details at the end of that time. One result of this size is that anyone going to buy, say a twenty-foot motor-cruiser should do some homework. Get hold of one or more of the yachting magazines before visiting the Show, and see which stands have boats of this size and type. The magazines all produce special issues for the Show, some produce several specials. These issues have both advertisements and extensive editorial coverage of the Show, and this enables a buyer to work out which stands he must visit.

If you intend to buy at the Show, it is a good idea to write to each firm beforehand and reserve two times for viewing their Show boat. This is because so many people go to the Show that exhibitors can only take over individual boats those people who have made appointments. It is possible to arrive at the Show and find that the time at which you would like to view is already booked.

Admittedly serious buyers are given all possible opportunity to view boats, but a previous appointment is well worth the small trouble of a letter. But make two appointments, because at the Show there will be a fair hubbub, which makes it hard to make up one's mind. Also some boats are very like others. So plenty of time to compare is needed, before signing a cheque.

The Show is such an event that some clubs charter buses and planes, to get their members to Earls Court. Whichever way you travel, if you want actually to buy, as opposed to browse round, it is advisable to get in promptly at 10 am. The middle of the day is usually not too crowded, till about 5 pm after which it gets increasingly difficult to conduct business. Saturday tends to be hopeless, with milling crowds pressing in solid down the aisles.

The Boat Show is a good place to buy certain types, such as outboard runabouts, racing dinghies, small cruisers of all types. In fact any popular type is well represented most years. But there can be surprising exceptions. One year there was virtually no choice of 5-ton auxiliary sloops.

On the other hand it is not a very satisfactory place to buy a boat over 10 tons, apart from certain lines of fibre-glass boats. The reason for this is that most boats, especially over 7 tons, tend to take 6 months to build. If a boat is ordered at the Show it is therefore unlikely to be delivered before July, maybe later if plans have to be prepared. This is rather later in the season than most people want.

However builders are aware of this problem, and they do what they can to alleviate it. The firms which turn out fibre-glass boats can normally offer less than 6 months delivery. Builders in wood sometimes lay down a hull as a speculation. Boats up to about 10 tons are often built by series production methods, a sort of semi mass-production. The production line throws off a boat every two or four weeks, or days. Builders who work this way can normally offer delivery in less than 6 months, otherwise they would not be at the Show. And it is noteworthy that builders of craft up to 50 tons are adapting series production techniques.

One corollary of this is that if you want to buy a boat at the Show, especially a big one, it is advisable to get there as early as possible, certainly before the first Saturday. On the other hand, be a little hesitant about signing. One wretched buyer, swept off his feet by the bright lights and delightful atmosphere, signed a buyer's form, and then regretted doing so. It cost him a reputed £1,500 to get out of the contract! And they say that boatbuilders are fuddy-duddies in business! In fairness to the industry I would say that this type of penalty clause is unusual. Although the boat-building industry is swinging towards the motor industry, with its unpleasantly excessive and overbearing salesmanship, on the whole it remains a friendly business. Most of the companies are small, many run by families, and virtually all the people in the boatbuilding side, particularly at executive level, are keen yachtsmen.

It has long been a taunt that boatbuilders are hopelessly inefficient individually and collectively. The annual success, and general slickness of the Boat Show belies this. It is run by the Ship and Boatbuilders National Federation and the *Daily Express*, but each individual stand is the product of the firm showing there. There is seldom a dud stand.

On the whole the Show does not vary much year by year. That is to say the overall pattern is fairly constant, though of course the boats, gadgets and diversions change annually. The beginner looking for a class dinghy will find one particularly valuable feature. Some of the big, powerful racing classes have stands of their own, or share part of a stand with a builder who specialises in their type of boat. This is a fine opportunity to learn where a given class is sailed, meet people who sail this type of boat, find out if they think it is within your capabilities, and perhaps fix up a trial sail. One thing about a small boat, it can be trailed down to the water easily at anytime of the year and put afloat for an hour or two. One word of warning. Members of a class, especially a racing class, are fanatics in defence of their own breed of boat. They know that nothing

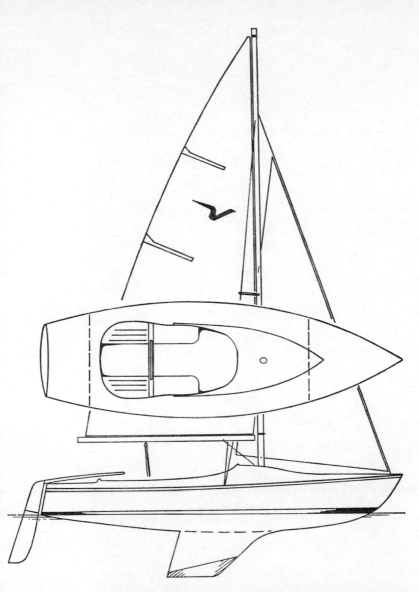

The 'Squib' is the smaller sister of the 'Ajax', both being designed by Oliver Lee of Burnham on Crouch, Essex. Both classes are for day racing, day sailing, family picnicing, maybe the occasional overnight short cruise and for teaching people to sail. 'Squib' is built of fibreglass and is 19' long, 17' 3" on the waterline, 6' 2" wide and draws 3' 3".

succeeds like success. The bigger classes get good press reports, and the more members they have the more powerful and wealthy the class Organisation becomes. So each class tries by fair means and gamesmanship to get as many people to join as possible.

A particularly valuable aspect of the Show is that no boat may be exhibited which does not have the official approval as to its standard of construction, if it is below 20 feet. Official approval is only given by the Ship and Boatbuilders National Federation when a boat is built to a certain minimum standards. Planking, frames and so on must be up to a minimum thickness for a given job.

Yet another side of the Show is that second-hand boats can be bought, as some brokers have stands. They usually have files (and files) of the particulars of different yachts, together with plans and photographs. Other stands are taken by sail-makers, spar-makers and the engine companies. This means that anyone buying a new or second-hand boat has an unequalled opportunity to compare different products and to see the actual equipment, which is so much easier to comprehend than when it is merely described on a leaflet. This is also an opportunity to talk to the manufacturers.

It is usual for people buying new boats or altering boats just bought to defer decisions about such matters as the exact choice of a new engine till the various alternatives have been inspected at the Show. One result of this is that some manufacturers now offer discounts for people who place orders in the autumn, otherwise there tends to be a very slack period till early January. Sail-makers in particular offer 5% or 10% autumn discount for orders placed between about mid-August and mid-October. This incidentally is another good reason for buying a boat in the autumn rather than the spring. It gives the buyer a chance to take advantage of this sort of discount.

'Cobra' designed by Jack Knight is a good example of a lightweight light-displacement racing keelboat which can be built at relatively low cost.

One trouble about ordering gear for a boat at the Show is that the supplier may be inundated with orders, and be late in delivering in the spring. There is thus a case to be made for ordering equipment before the rush of Show orders.

As to whether or not the Show is a good place to buy a new boat there are powerful arguments on both sides. The Show is carefully cooked up, with some skill and undoubted success, to be a glamorous pageant. Motoring correspondents forever moan that the Motor Show is dreary when compared to the Boat Show. This means there is seldom a calm detached atmosphere for buying a boat. Also a boat at the show is usually glossed up till she shines superbly. 'Show finish' is a well-known phrase, and this surface gloss can be misleading. It takes knowledge and experience to judge a boat's ability and worth under the bright lights. She should be imagined clawing desperately off a rocky lee shore in a good noisy gale, with the wind blowing force 8, gusting 10, a seasick crew, the night as dark as a politician's soul, raining, cold, hellish. How then would this glittering, chromium plated, dolled-up bit of a boat perform? If you have the strength of mind to look coolly at the boat you propose to buy, then the Show is not a dangerous place for you.

Suppose, however, that even away from the Show you lack the knowledge and ability to assess one boat as compared with another rather similar. Here the Show again provides a valuable service. There are each year four or five experts, who sit at desks on a special stand, offering advice free. The more conscientious of these fellows will go round the show and pick out good and doubtful boats. Their advice costs nothing, and may be just what is wanted.

Up to now the word 'show' has meant the London Boat Show. There are other, lesser shows, each year. Cities throughout the world, not always those near the sea, have their annual shows. In Britain boat shows are held annually, or bi-annually in several cities. They are held inland and near the coast, on both sides of the Irish border, and sometimes in quite small towns where they

Boat shows are occasionally combined with caravan and camping shows. These smaller shows are all a long way short of the London Show, and seldom do they include yachts over 6 tons.

Another form of boat show is an annual jamboree staged by a big chandler or boat retailer. These events are usually timed for early spring, and are local in character. Again boats up to but seldom over 6 tons are shown. The arena is sometimes just the normal showroom, sometimes it is extended to a car-park or similar open space. The main value to the buyer of these events is that it gives a chance to compare ashore a variety of small cruisers, dinghies and so on.

4   *Deliveries*

One very good reason for not buying a boat at another yachting centre is the cost of bringing her home. There are two basic methods of getting a yacht back to her new home port – either by land or on her own bottom. Occasionally boats are sent round the coast on small freighters. In certain special circumstances this can be very economical. One has to include the cost of loading and off-loading, but where the ship's own derricks can be used this is usually a very small matter.

Relatively few boats are moved by rail, partly because they have to be put on to the railway carriage and this usually means at least a short journey by road and then, on arrival, again transferred to a lorry before being put in the water. However, plenty of harbours, indeed the majority of commercial harbours, have ample facilities for moving railway wagons close to the water's edge under cranes and, in theory at least, there is no reason why a boat should not be sent from harbour to harbour by rail. The cost can be competitive but the insurance should be very carefully detailed. Indeed, the main objection to moving by rail is the exceptionally high risk of damage to the boat.

Moving by lorry is often the cheapest way, particularly for vessels between 18 ft and 40 ft overall, both power and sail. Usually the cheapest method of moving boats under 18 ft or even more is on a trailer behind a car, particularly where the boat has its own trailer. It often pays to hire a trailer specially for the delivery trip. Ideally, one should use a trailer specially tailored to the boat. Craft up to about 14 ft or, in special circumstances, up to 18 ft, can be moved on top of a car, provided there is a suitable rack.

Deliveries by sea under tow should be avoided. Yachts were never intended by God or man to be towed and they seem to know it. Long distance towing involves multiple and sometimes extraordinary, problems and accidents.

Every year many boats are moved around the coast from centre to centre under their own power when they change hands. Quite a little industry has been built up so that the yachting magazines now have under the classified columns a list headed 'Yacht Deliveries'. The firms advertising quote prices which vary according to the size of the vessel and the distance to be delivered.

As with everything else in the yachting sphere, the cheapest delivery quotation is not necessarily the best value.

The wise owner wishing to move his boat to her new home port will obtain quotations from two or three delivery firms, possibly more. In the absence of personal recommendation from other yachtsmen, it is possible to gauge the experience and competence of a delivery firm by the questions asked in connection with the quotation. A good firm will have had a lot of experience and it will want to know the quantity and quality of safety gear on the yacht, also the fullest information about navigation gear, whether the yacht has a dinghy and so on. They will also ask for exact instructions as to the precise location of the yacht, who is in charge of her, where the cabin key is to be found and so on.

Any experienced yacht delivery crew will tell you that the boats in their charge often fall into one of two categories. Either the boat is brand new, in which case she will have the inevitable teething troubles of a new boat, or she will be an old boat in need of a full refit. Owners tend to be conscienceless about employing delivery crews to bring back ill-equipped yachts which have, perhaps, been neglected for some time, possibly laid up on a mud flat and left there, with dubious gear and worn out sails, siezed engine, rusty anchor-chain, and so on. The owner plans a full and thorough refit, perhaps doing much of the work himself just as soon as the boat reaches her new home port. However, this is too late and it is very unfair to expect delivery crews to bring a boat back prior to her complete fitting-out.

It is particularly important that the boat should be

fully overhauled before she sets out on a delivery trip, because this journey will often be in the early spring or late autumn (when many boats change hands), with the weather at its most vicious. Often enough the yacht will have spent the whole of her previous life gently pottering around the coast for short distances. Now she is expected to drive hard to windward in deep water for several days on end. Delivery trips are often the toughest voyages in a boat's career and it is distressing how often delivery crews are forced to set out with a boat that has not reached a reasonable standard of seaworthiness.

A yacht bought six or seven hundred miles from her home port all too often cannot be brought home by her new owner because of the time involved. But where possible it is well worth while for the new owner to undertake the job because he will learn a lot more about his boat on a long, tough passage than in thousands of quiet weekends exploring well protected creeks.

Time is the limiting factor for most people. However a boat pushed hard with a strong crew can be expected to average about 100 miles every 24 hours under sail. This basic figure applies to yachts between 6–16 tons. The smaller yacht will fall back in bad weather, but unless the bigger yacht has ample crew she will tend to be relatively not so much faster, and 100 miles per 24 hours is a useful and usually fairly safe basic average.

Power yachts should not be expected to achieve more than 75% of their top speed over a long passage. In this connection the seller's quoted top speed should be ignored, since it will invariably be over-optimistic.

Where the yacht is delivered by land or sea, by the owner or by a professional delivery crew, or just a bunch of the owner's friends, it is essential that the insurance underwriters are fully informed. They need to know the port of departure and arrival, dates, who is in charge and so on. Also a CG66 form should be filled in. This is obtainable from the Coastguards and is sent to them on completion, so that they keep an eye on the yacht. It is a sensible precaution whenever a coastwise passage is being made and incidentally costs nothing.

5 *Matching boat with owner*

A boat should match her owner's temperament, experience, family and his funds. It is all too easy to let money dominate the choice of boat.

For instance, a man who is hard up finds he can only afford a small open boat. Studying yachting magazines suggests that there is little choice except between racing sailing dinghies of various classes, and small outboard runabouts. And for a man who prefers the quietness, adventure, and voyaging which make up cruising, these types completely fail to satisfy. It is tempting to buy what is easily available, whereas the correct course is to re-examine the market.

There is no reason why a would-be owner who wants to cruise should not do so in either a sailing dinghy or a small open motor-boat. The literature of this type of cruising is thin and open-boat cruising seldom gets headlines in yachting magazines, so that the general yachting public are scarcely aware of its existence.

For a start, someone keen to get into yachting should talk to as many owners as possible. This will show the diversity and variety of different types of sport afloat. Each owner will be quite fanatically enthusiastic about his own branch of the sport. Plenty will offer trips just to demonstrate how superb their own craft is. Each champions his own type of yachting. This can be a bit confusing: there is no denying that water-skiing is thrilling, dinghy racing (when there are slashing fast planes) is hard to beat, cruising up quiet, distant backwaters on a late summer's evening is sheer bliss, especially after a too-hectic week's work, yet who can remain placid during the glorious, roarious, thunderous start of a motor-boat race. And so on. It is a multitudinous sport, and each branch is far separated from many of the others.

When you have discussed the different types of

yachting with as many of the highly biased owners as possible, the next call should be to a broker for a second-hand boat, or a designer if a new boat is wanted. He should be open-minded unless he is one of the fairly rare specialists. One trouble here is that the broker will seldom sell very small boats, and if he does he may not have either a wide experience or a wide choice to offer. Which designer? A good basic rule is that a designer who lives in a given area will know the requirements of the local waters, and so provide the best boat for his own district.

A married man should consult with his wife about buying a boat, even if he normally ignores her to a greater or lesser extent. It is worth remembering this: The few people who give up yachting are almost all victims of their own over-enthusiasm. They have given up yachting because their wives hate yachts. The vast majority of women in this category have been pitch-forked too roughly into a tough sport. They have been thrust without warning into small cramped boats, in the middle of a black, blustery rainy evening, without the inner comfort of a hot meal, wearing fashionable but ineffective oilskins. It is no wonder they are unlimitedly miserable.

Take a tip from a young yard managing director I know. He has built up a successful business in five years, starting with little more than an overdraft and his own determination. He says:

'Selling boats is not that difficult. You take the measurements of the best cooker in the Simpson-Lawrence catalogue. You design a good, comfortable galley round this big stove, then you design your boat round the galley. This sells the boat to the owner's wife, and she sells the boat to him.'

While it is preposterous to generalise about women, it is certain that a lot of them look upon all yachts which are larger than dinghies as a kind of week-end cottage. They want comfort above all else, and appear to define this elusive quality this way:

A dry protected corner in the cockpit or on deck,

Attractive features on this Mylne designed motor-sailer are the convenient dinghy stowage in davits aft (called 'feathers'); the ratlines up the mast, and the mast in a tabernacle for easy amateur maintenance.

This rig is especially suitable for a motor-sailer and includes a partially fully battened mainsail and a genoa of generous area. The latter would be lowered in freshening winds.

where they are well sheltered but can see what is going on.

As much dryness down below as possible, which means a tight deck.

Headroom in the galley, or a good seat in the galley from which all cooking operations can be conducted.

A separate enclosed toilet compartment with full headroom.

Full headroom for dressing, which may acceptably be in the toilet compartment if it is large enough.

These are the basic requirements, but the more assets

in the way of enhanced comfort that can be seen aboard a boat, the more chance a man has of selling the idea of a purchase to his wife. I remember helping in the buying of a fairly large yacht, and the would-be owner was no fool. He was taking a lot of trouble to make sure his wife liked the yacht before he parted with his money.

She said: 'Can we carry a car on the deck?'

He turned to me and said: 'Can we?'

I said: 'Yes, a small one.'

So he said to her: 'Yes, dear, a small one. Say an Aston Martin.'

And that helped to clinch the deal. I had the sense not to quibble about whether an Aston can be called a small car. I just made sure the aft deck beams would carry the load.

A boat for a family must, above all, be within the weight of the available muscle-power. If a yacht is too big for the owner, his wife and children, then it will run away with them. They will find that they cannot sheet in the headsails or cannot douse the mainsail. If she is a power yacht, they may learn too late they cannot warp her alongside against a stiff breeze. However, this sort of problem can be eased enormously by the correct application of power. More, or bigger, sheet and halliard winches, a power windlass and maybe power to lift the dinghy on board can transform a yacht. These days there is a choice of hydraulic and electric winches which can do a lot of work at the press of a button. They cost between about £60 and £250, or more, according to the size and horsepower. This is not a lot when compared with the total cost of a yacht. It can mean that an otherwise unsuitable yacht can be made manageable for a particular family.

There are two limitations to this way of making a yacht right for a family. Power winches cannot be used on yachts below 8 tons except in special circumstances. Also, if the power fails there must be alternative ways of getting the job done.

Very powerful sheet winches work wonders, but there must still be some muscle to operate these winches.

A nine-year-old boy, provided he is experienced and not tired or seasick, can sheet in quite well if he is behind a really good winch. A six-year-old is not really much help. And for children new to yachting, even a twelve-year-old is not much good the first season.

All this boils down to the fact that for a family a motor-sailer (sometimes called a 50/50) is best for most families. The older, tougher and keener the children, the more sail can be carried. This is doubly true, as more sail means more to do, and less chance for the children to get bored. These days the best motor-sailers are shaped to sail well. In many cases they are just good all-round, comfortable cruisers with powerful, but not necessarily massive or obtrusive engines, and plenty of fuel tank capacity.

Some men go sailing specifically to get away from women. It is my observation that this type of owner is best suited by either a fairly extreme type of racing dinghy, or a racing boat which has the accent on stark efficiency and speed. The dinghy should be one which is a popular wide-spread, tough class, with distant meetings week-end after week-end, all over the country, so that the dinghy is trailed hither and yon, never racing on the same water two week-ends running. The larger cabined boat should sacrifice comfort for speed to such an extent that the owner and his all-male crew are glad to get back to home comforts on Sunday night.

The same sort of considerations apply to men who do dull sedentary jobs all week. They usually fit in best with a boat that gives them all the excitement their jobs lack. This is not a universal rule. There are certain people who by temperament cannot abide that lurching from crisis to crisis which constitutes tough cruising or racing in light, extreme yachts. This type of man is happy pottering about in a garden. For him probably the best boat is a very old one, which needs constant care and maintenance. A man with creative instincts, whose job gives no outlet to his ability, is often content to work away repairing and rebuilding almost every month of the year.

There used to be a character at Burnham who owned an old fishing boat, converted to a yacht. He only went to sea one week each year, and the rest of the time he worked away, enjoying himself hugely. Though his boat was probably not originally all that well built, she always glistened and had a beautiful groomed appearance. He was happy, and that is all that matters.

It could be argued that not everyone has the skill of hand to work away on a boat, and achieve good results. The answer to this must be that very few people are lacking in ability and dexterity. They just need practice. Besides, the boat-owner needs so many skills, from sign-writing to decorative rope-work, from canvas-work to joinery, that everyone should be able to enjoy the kind of yachting which comes under the heading of 'pottering about'.

For many people, the only boat is one that races. Here, the golden rule is to buy into the local class. Fortunately, most clubs run at least three or four classes, so that there is a choice to suit different owners. It will usually be found that each class has its own local captain or secretary. A talk with him will be rewarding, as it will show up the kind of people who race in the class. Some classes, notably those used in the Olympic games, the faster, lighter planing dinghies, and the expensive restricted classes attract the wealthy, the fanatically keen, the type of owner who selects his crew for their experience and leaves ashore wives and family regardless. Older classes tend to be more favoured by family men, partly because they are cheaper, partly because the atmosphere afloat is less cut-throat, more friendly. Some racing classes quite clearly can only take a crew of two. Others, usually ballasted half-deckers, can carry one or two children, as well as the parents, and still win.

Racing dinghies come in every shape, size and price bracket. The smallest is about 10 ft minimum length, and about £40 minimum cost second-hand. The largest is about 20 ft long, and around £600 complete with all the trimmings. However, it sometimes happens that a particular club only races one or two classes which are not so dissimilar. It may be that your local club has a fleet of Finn single-handers and another of 14 ft Internationals. Neither would suit a relative beginner aged over 40 and out of training. This is an instance where it would be a mistake to buy into a local class. It is better to motor 20 miles or more to the next club, and buy a GP14 or a Mirror or some such. This extra motoring every week-end will be well worthwhile in the extra enjoyment afloat. After a few seasons, with increasing experience and know-how, it might make sense to move into the nearer club, with their more extreme types of dinghy. But it will probably be a mistake to move until this particular owner can regularly win in his own class.

Once a particular type of boat has been selected, it is best to get hold of all available books and magazine articles on this particular line.

Public libraries subscribe to some yachting magazines and usually keep back numbers, which means that a boat buyer can work back through past issues and pick up a lot of information.

When all is said and done, it is often the money available which dictates the final choice. As a rough guide it is best to spend only 85% of the available funds on the yacht, whether it be new or second-hand, power or sail. If everything is poured into the initial purchase price, there will be nothing left over for modifications and unexpected problems. Besides, money should be retained for insurance, for contingencies, such as the discovery that the anchor chain is too short for normal cruising, for that breakage early in the season caused by not knowing the boat, and her little quirks.

If yachtsman have anything in common, it is a tendency to buy bigger than they can afford. This applies not only at schoolboy level, but also at millionaire level.

6　*Red herrings*

Red herrings cause people to buy unsuitable boats. They are temptations which afflict almost every yachtsman several times a year. They occur at all levels from little boys to tycoons. It is all too easy for somebody to talk himself into buying a large, powerful, ultra-fast racing dinghy when he would have much more fun out of a slightly more modest one-design boat. The one-design dinghy might be slower, won't be an Olympic Class, may not receive so much attention from the yachting press, but it will suit the average dinghy racing man very much better than an *extreme* racing machine.

At the other end of the scale, a very wealthy owner will visualize himself basking in the Carribean sun aboard a massive, multi-engined yacht. He visualizes three high-speed tenders swinging at the boat booms, the private hovercraft, the six paid hands, the acres of scrubbed teak decks, the twin radar scanners and so on. But what is the point of having this kind of boat a whole day and a half away by air if his fourteen factories never let him get away for more than a Saurday afternoon and a Sunday? Much better have a sensible cruiser at a nearby harbour, only two hours away in the Bentley. He will get many more hours aboard and for his annual holiday he can charter somebody else's expensive load of sea-going trouble, on sunny seas 4,000 miles from home.

A very common mistake is to buy an out and out ocean racer where there is no intention of doing a full intense season's ocean racing. The typical owner, with wife and two or three children, who cruises for 22 weekends a year and races in four offshore events, would find more satisfaction in a cruiser that rates well but is not extreme, rather than an unmitigated ocean racer. Modern ocean racers become yearly more specialised, more highly tuned, more costly, and more demanding on owners and crew.

For anyone wanting a dinghy which can be carried on top of a car, the Gull has much to recommend it. It is 11 ft. long and can be bought complete or in kit form from Small Craft, of Blockley, Gloucestershire. This boat is an inexpensive all-rounder.

A good general-purpose family sailing dinghy is the 14 ft. Leader. It may be bought complete, or partly assembled, or as a kit of parts from Small Craft, of Blockley, Gloucestershire. This boat will take an outboard, and can be rowed.

Obtainable in both fibreglass and plywood, the 15 ft. 10 ins. Wayfarer is a powerful dinghy, suitable for rougher waters than most small open boats. This boat is easy to trail behind a car, yet has space aboard for two people to go camping/cruising. Among the builders are Small Craft, of Blockley, Gloucestershire.

The 420 class is a worldwide one, and one of the biggest in numbers. This 13 ft. 9 ins. glassfibre racing dinghy provides high performance sport in light winds and strong conditions. British builders are Honnor Marine, of Seymour Wharf, Totnes, Devon. Like many boats, this type can be bought by hire-purchase.

Designed for the owner who wants to combine racing with family cruising, the Lazy E is 15 ft. long. It is built by Jack Holt Ltd, of The Embankment, Putney, London. Two versions are available but this is a one-design, intended for even racing, especially in fairly open waters.

One of the fastest growing dinghy classes is the Mirror. Many of these boats are amateur built, using a simple technique. This boat, which can be rowed, sailed or outboard-driven, is 10 ft. 10 ins. long and has a beam of 4 ft. 7 ins. Details from: *Daily Mirror*, Holborn, London.

Failte is an unusual family cruiser, designed by A. Mylne and Co., of Royal Terrace, Glasgow. For easy handling she has a ketch rig, but the usual lower efficiency of this rig has been overcome by fitting full length battens in the main and mizzen.

The two-berth 19 ft. Mastiff was designed by Colin Mudie for amateur or professional builders. Engines up to about 120 h.p. will give speeds in the range of 15 to 25 knots. Further details can be obtained from the designer at Bywater Lodge, Pierside, Lymington, Hants.

The other absurd yearning is to go long-distance ocean cruising when there is no more than a fortnight's holiday a year available. It makes no sense to buy an ocean cruising type for weekending. For a start, the deep-sea cruiser usually has a small, cramped cockpit, whereas the weekender wants a bit of space for himself, wife and children. By all means have a self-draining cockpit, there is no better safety precaution; by all means have thick, high cockpit coamings, but go for a bit of space inside these coamings. Too often ocean cruisers are under-canvassed and under-engined which means that they won't sail well in light airs, and they have not enough horsepower to get them home against the tide in time for work on Monday morning.

In the motor-boat field, red herrings lead to buying a boat that goes unnecessarily fast. Apart from the fact that high speed boats are expensive to run, uncomfortable in moderate weather and pure hell in bad weather, they tend to depreciate fast. Worst of all, they cover the whole of the local cruising ground in one weekend, leaving nowhere nearby to explore for subsequent weekends.

As a general rule, the red herring leads a buyer into getting a boat which is too big for him. It is true that increased size means more speed and more comfort, but a boat that's too big soon becomes a liability. Yachting is only fun if it is well within the financial means of everybody involved. The trouble with red herrings is they lure buyers into getting boats which are not only unsuitable for most of the year's sailing, but also too expensive for the owner concerned. It is worth remembering the famous yachting phrase: 'the smaller the boat, the greater the fun.' This saying was certainly invented by Noah.

The source of many red herrings are the yachting magazines. They tend to glamorise certain types, certain races and the exploits of some people. The advertisements further stress these successes and achievements. From year to year the object of this glamorisation varies. It may be the One-ton Cup, the Admiral's Cup, the

America's Cup, the Olympic Games, the Single-handed Transatlantic Race, the Round-Britain Race, the Trans-pacific Race, the Sydney–Hobart Race, the Cowes–Torquay Powerboat Race or any other event which catches the imagination and enthusiasm of the yachting magazines' editorial staff.

That is not to say that these major yachting events are not important. They are. They are exciting, at times wildly thrilling and they are responsible for the produc-tion of the majority of the finest yachts in their own particular field. The trouble is they set everybody pipe-dreaming. A man with money in his pocket and the intention of buying can be so easily misled by all the excitement into getting the wrong boat.

The sum total of all this is to take a long, hard look at what the boat you are about to buy has got to do. It is not a bad idea to see what other boats are kept on the same moorings as the one you will use. Find out which boats are being regularly used weekend after weekend without changing hands for many years. Remember, too, that this year's glamour type may look very out-dated in three years time. In short, take a hard-headed, cold appraisal of what your true needs are and don't be misled by the current excitement in the press.

7   *Buying a small sailing cruiser*

In this instance, let us agree that by small we mean cruisers under 24 ft *overall* length. It would be a fair generalisation to say that in the last twenty years very few poor boats over 5 tons have been produced, but in the smaller sizes this is not, alas, true.

There is a wide choice of these small boats, as a glance at two or three yachting magazines will show. They vary from mass-produced boats, which come from factories, down to special local products usually designed with special local conditions in mind.

When you buy a racing dinghy, a main consideration is the importance of buying into a local class. This does not apply with a cruiser and so the choice is almost infinite, except in the rare case where the cruiser is to be raced in a local one-design cruiser class like the Stellas. In practice there is a great deal of cruiser racing done almost everywhere, but almost invariably this is on handicap basis.

Far and away the most important attribute to seek is good ability to windward in bad weather. This is where most of the poor boats are inadequate, if not downright dangerous.

A boat of this type must have stability, which is produced by ample beam and plenty of ballast. However beam cannot be increased too much otherwise the boat becomes so bluff she will not go to windward against a rough sea. This makes it doubly important to see that there is ample weight hanging well down on the end of a good fin, or pair of fins.

Owners of inefficient boats tend to find out they are dud under embarrassing circumstances, and so these boats come on the market at depressed prices. This means that a would-be buyer can detect which classes are to be avoided if he takes a bit of trouble. By working through plenty of yachting magazines, through column after column of classified advertisements, it is not too difficult to discern which classes of boats come on the market heavily depreciated after one or two years of life. These are the classes to avoid.

It is inevitable that most people looking for a small cruiser will be doing so mainly because they are short of money. It has already been established that only 85% of available funds should be spent on a boat, but for this type of yacht it is more important to have seaworthiness than reserve funds. In short, price should not dictate the choice. This is a case where the biggest possible boat should be bought, even if it means getting extra money from the bank, H.P. company, or even, as a last resort, working for it.

This business of stability naturally only matters in bad weather. But then, most of our troubles come upon us in winds over Force 6. This is when the crew get really seasick, sails tear, engines won't start and breakages occur. It is no good having a fat insurance policy and all sorts of excellent equipment if the boat is just not able to claw off the lee shore. What makes the stability doubly important is that small boats have less draft than their bigger sisters. Consequently, the keels are not permanently deep down in solid water. As a wave breaks under the hull the whole boat lurches to leeward. If, at the same time, the boat is heeling a lot, then she will not even make good a course 90° to the wind, let alone claw off the shore.

There is a strong case for increasing the keel weight on a lot of these small cruisers, even on some of the best built. Unfortunately it is not sufficient just to add weight. Considerable additional stiffening is required to take care of the extra stresses.

In parenthesis, it is worth remembering that some of the mass-produced cruisers have had their keel weights increased when production of the Mark I version has stopped and the Mark II started. This is an admission indeed, so above all avoid the Mark I types and look long and hard at the Mark IIs before buying.

These small boats are often built with twin bilge keels,

and sometimes offered with alternative single or twin keels. There are plenty of arguments for and against twin keels. It is perfectly true that anyone who keeps a boat in a shoal area will find twin keels are a great advantage, since the boat sits upright when aground. This type is also slightly easier to put on a trailer or haul up. However, the main trouble will be to find a boat with adequate performance and there is no gainsaying the fact that single fin boats go better than twin keelers. Plenty of arguments have been produced trying to prove the opposite, but if twin keels were more efficient then they would be used in hot racing classes. In practice there is no instance of a successful racing machine being fitted with twin fixed keels. The bilge-board scow is not the same sort of creature at all. She is a vast flat planing dinghy, and she has two centre-boards, not fixed fins. She raises the windward board too, so making herself a single fin boat when beating.

A twin keel boat is certainly recommended for a cruising ground like those parts of the Thames Estuary, where the yacht lies aground between tides. In this region the tides run so strongly that small cruisers must anyhow be sailed down tide as much as possible, if sailing is not to become a dreary slog against the current. Using the tides intelligently is very often a substitute for windward ability in this type of sailing area. Even here, if racing is contemplated, then either a single fin or a good handicap is needed.

This continual harping on bad weather arises because virtually any boat is safe and comfortable until the wind really pipes up. And even in strong winds in really sheltered waters it is rare to get into much trouble. So if the cruising ground is to be in narrow waters, on the Broads for instance, or up a river, then this insistence on weatherly ability is nothing like so important.

A possible way of alleviating the problem of poor performance is to fit an inboard engine of adequate power. Five horsepower is normally enough to push a small cruiser against a strong breeze. Coupled with a well-reefed main and storm jib, it will force her to windward against severe conditions. One of the great advantages of running an engine as well as sails is that the chance of a mis-tack is virtually eliminated.

On a very small cruiser, say 17 ft on the waterline, even a three-horsepower engine used with well-reefed sails can deal with extraordinarily bad conditions.

Ideally, one would go for a small diesel engine, provided the boat can carry the weight, because these units tend to be so reliable. A serious cruising owner puts up with the extra diesel noise because he is quite happy to turn the engine off whenever he can sail without it. When the weather is bad and he is using the engine, the robust noise can be very heartening.

Many of these small cruisers carry outboard engines but these seem to be unsatisfactory in bad weather. For a start, they tend to have trouble through propeller emergence above the waterline in rough water. As the propeller comes up to the surface, it races wildly which damages the engine. An outboard does not like to operate when the boat is heeled, yet in particularly bad conditions it is surprising how a *combination* of sail and power will produce useful progress, whereas one or other alone is inadequate.

One good thing about these small mass-produced cruisers, is that there are so many of them, it is usually easy to find an owner of one who will give you a trial spin. Alternatively, the factory producing them may offer a trial. The ideal is to have an extensive trial lasting more than one day away from sheltered waters, in Force 5 or 6 winds. No one voluntarily sets out in Force 7 or 8 in these small cruisers.

A boat of this size must inevitably be cramped inside. There is a great temptation to buy the boat with the most headroom. It is better to remember that headroom is only used for twenty or thirty minutes every 24 hours. Headroom is usually a disadvantage from almost every point of view, in that it raises the weight and windage of the deck and deck structure, the deck fittings, and so on. If headroom is wanted, the answer is very often to fit a big hatch, if necessary with side curtains, so that it can be opened even in the rain. Provided it is made properly with deep coamings all round, it should be reasonably watertight.

Finally, when buying this size of cruiser, remember that it is often a stepping stone to a bigger yacht. So without letting this consideration dominate the choice, it is worth investigating the ease with which a chosen boat can be resold.

8   *A boat for the beginner - Sail*

Most people will agree that the beginner's boat has these basic requirements:

1. Cheapness – because it is usually soon changed for a more advanced yacht.
2. Toughness – to stand up to the bumps and other mistakes.
3. Safety – obviously.
4. It must be interesting to sail – but not exciting; this comes later. When learning, the novelty of being afloat is enough, provided the boat is not absurdly under-canvassed. She should be an adequate performer, but planing and acute sensitivity at the helm are refinements which the beginner can well do without.
5. Suitable for single-handed sailing – because practice is what every beginner needs. Once the learner has had a little tuition he will most certainly want to spend as much time as possible afloat. This will be difficult if he has to wait for a crew, so once he has a moderate degree of confidence, he should be able to go out in settled weather, in sheltered waters, on his own.
6. Good all-round visibility. Any boat which has a window in the mainsail or jib is suspect. Of course, a low cut headsail can always be altered, or another jib borrowed or bought for the learner's use. But a high standing cuddy or small cabin which limits forward visibility is a nuisance, if not dangerous. Admittedly this, too, can be altered or, alternatively, the helmsman's seat raised.
7. Good manners, While every owner wants a boat which is not excessively 'weather helmy', for a beginner it is really important. 'Good manners' covers a very wide field. For instance some yachts

have weather helm initially, then lee helm as they heel, and some even revert to weather helm once the deck edge is under. This is disconcerting for an experienced helmsman, while for a beginner it could lead to all sorts of troubles.

8. Of a size to suit sailing waters. For a small lake a big boat is unsuitable, whereas for the open sea it is better to have a little extra length and beam to cope with the sterner conditions. In any case, 10 ft long is about the smallest basic size since this provides only adequate room for the beginner and his instructor. For anyone more than 35 years old, even 12 ft long is rather small, particularly for open sea work. At the other end of the scale, 20 ft long, or maybe at the most, 24 ft is an advisable top limit. Over this size sails become large unless the boat is hopelessly undercanvassed and dreary to sail in light airs.

9. A 'Day Sailer' type. It is much better to learn to sail first and leave cruising and racing for later. Both cruising and racing involve a variety of special techniques. There is navigation, pilotage, weather lore, anchoring, and a thousand other things involved. The best plan seems to be to learn to handle the boat and make her go the way you want first.

Having decided on the basic requirements, we now look around and discover, with some dismay, that practically nobody builds boats for beginners. When I realised this a few years ago, I developed the Morag Class, just for this job. These boats are not one-design and can be of any normal construction, decked or undecked, and even have a little cabin. They soon attained some popularity and I was asked to produce larger and smaller versions, which resulted in the 18 ft Morag Major and the 12 ft 6 ins Mini-Morag.

For children there is the Cadet class which is 10 ft 6 ins long, but these are a little cramped for adults. One of their main advantages is that they are raced as a regular one-design class at quite a number of centres all over the world, and they have an annual regatta week on

Burnham-on-Crouch which now has an international status. Other boats, which like the Cadet are hard chine, of ply, are the Gull and Heron Classes (l.o.a. 11 ft) and the two types sponsored by the *Daily Mirror*, the 16 footer and the 10 ft 6 ins Mirror class.

Occasionally, one comes across sturdy little 10 ft clinker boats which were Naval issue up to about 1940. Sailing versions of these boats were fitted with lugsails and $\frac{1}{4}$ in steel daggerboards. They make excellent beginners' boats and some can still be found around the coasts. The rowing version can be converted to sail and this may be the most inexpensive type available. But it is very important to be sure that the boat is the standard Naval type. Boats designed for rowing which have been made to sail often lack beam, sometimes have too much rise of floor and have usually too soft a turn of bilge for safe sailing.

Another popular type is the 11 ft scow found all round the Solent area and this has the advantage of being towable.

For an older person, especially somebody beginning to get a bit stiff in the limbs, a dinghy is not entirely suitable. Even if it is a very stable type which will not tip the learner into the water, it still needs fairly quick reactions. This type of person is probably better off with a ballasted boat; ideally, it should be of shallow draft for most waters. This means that the crew can push her off if she goes ashore without going overboard even up to the waist. They will be able to see the bottom very often before they touch. Also the absence of draft extends the cruising ground. To make the boat perfect, she should have a centreboard working down through the ballast keel. This gives improved performance to windward, warns the helmsman when he gets into shallow water and also teaches the techniques of centreboard sailing.

Alan Buchanan designed the 11-ton Queen Class which was developed in wood first then built in fibreglass. This is a typical cruiser-racer intended for family sailing and passage racing, and is the sort of yacht which can be expected to have a long useful life.

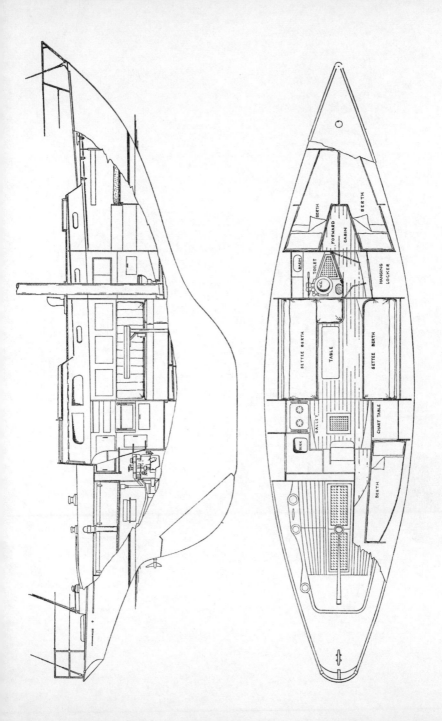

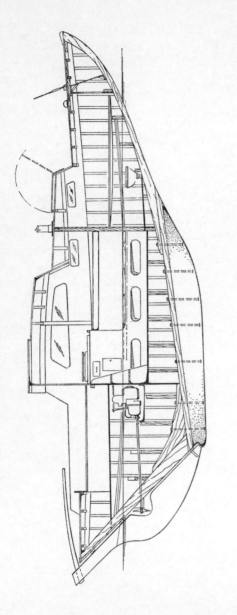
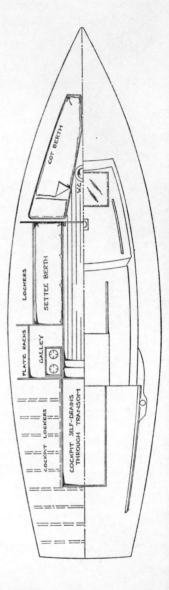

COT BERTH

W.C.

LOCKERS

PLATE RACKS

SETTEE BERTH

GALLEY

COCKPIT LOCKERS

COCKPIT SELF-DRAINS
THROUGH TRANSOM

This ideal boat also has a wide cockpit with comfortable seats and a moderately high coaming so that everybody is well down out of the way of most of the spray, nicely protected, located where they cannot be pitched out of the boat, and yet where they can see well all round. Such a boat will be extremely hard to find, like all good beginners' boats.

One way round the problem is to go to a sailing school. They normally run one-week courses and their address can be obtained from the Royal Yachting Association, 5 Lancaster Gate, London, SW1, or from the classified advertisements in the back of yachting magazines.

In passing, it is worth noting that beginners' boats are so difficult to find that some sailing schools use unsuitable boats. I even know of one using 12 ft Nationals on the open sea, which seems to me to be rather unsatisfactory. However, anybody who completes that course successfully can certainly claim to have acquired a useful measure of skill, even if they have been 'thrown in at the deep end'.

Owing to the difficulty of obtaining a really good beginner's boat, it is good sense to try and borrow or charter one instead of buying. It would be a good idea to see if the nearest sailing school will charter one of their boats when their season ends. Some stop running their courses fairly early in the year, around September, and may be only too pleased to obtain a modest extra income at this late period in the season. Chartering a boat has the added advantage that it does not have to be sold when a more advanced steed is required. If you can charter a boat from the sailing school where you have taken a course, then you will be used to their type of boat, which is an obvious advantage. Better still, charter

The Folkboat was originally designed by the Scandinavian Yacht Racing Union. It has been enormously successful and has been developed in many different ways. This version shows a much enlarged cabin-top, a fairly elaborate four-berth layout, and a well-protected cockpit. These plans show wood construction but Folkboats have been built in fibreglass. Dimensions are: 25′ overall, 19′ 6″ waterline, 7′ 2″ beam and 3′ 9″ draught, with 230 sq ft of working sail area.

two, one for yourself and one for your wife, girl-friend, son or whoever would go out with you. It is often, if not always, much better to put two beginners in two boats, rather than have them both in one boat.

Apart from any other considerations, two boats will inevitably result in impromptu races and nothing teaches competence, seamanship and getting the best out of a boat like racing.

Whenever a boat is used for a beginner, she should be intelligently equipped. There should be enough internal buoyancy to make her float high after flooding so that she can be bailed dry, even in bad weather when there is a sea running. However, there must not be so much buoyancy that she floats extremely high after a capsize and races off, down wind, lying on her side. Some dinghies do this, drifting faster than the crew in the water can swim after them. It is generally only the light, well-developed racing dinghy which behaves in this way.

Boats floating high in the water are not easy to get into and so a rope-ladder for re-boarding, kept coiled aft, is often an asset. It must be located where the man in the water can reach it and pull it down over the transom. Hang it low enough in the water for him to get a foot into the bottom rung without a desperate struggle. A keel boat should have enough buoyancy to float her, regardless of how much weight there is in the ballast.

The reefing gear should be foolproof, massive, and definitely not a delicate, sophisticated affair of high precision engineering which only works the day it leaves the factory and soon clogs with verdigris and deposited salt.

There should be an anchor permanently attached to a good terylene line. This line must have its inner end permanently secured and the length of the anchor rope should be five times the depth of water where the boat is likely to anchor.

A dry locker, preferably a completely watertight one, is needed for spare sweaters, sandwiches and daylight distress smoke signals.

There should be two at least of these distress signals; one may not work or, if it does, all the surrounding population may be inconsiderately looking the wrong way at the time. In theory, the beginner is never out at night so rockets and flares should not be necessary. However, it is often easier to attract attention at night, since rockets go high, whereas smoke flares often only show up a rather feeble trail of wispy orange close to the water. Boats get into trouble often enough when the crew are tired, as they may be in the evening after a long day afloat, so carry flares as well as the day signals.

9   *A boat for the beginner - Power*

Beginners inevitably make mistakes. For this reason a really reliable powerboat is needed. There will be quite enough adventures and excitement in the first few days without having to cope with a temperamental engine or a boat which is falling apart.

She should be stable too, though this does not mean she will be steady. In fact, I never knew a motorboat owner, and I do know hundreds, who did not complain once, or maybe ten times, a year that his boat rolled too much. The plain fact is that motorboats roll. Some people try and get over this by buying bigger boats, but there is a limit even for millionaires. If it is any small consolation, I know a few extremely wealthy powerboat owners and they too complain most bitterly about rolling. The complaints lessen after they have spent £2,000 or more on roll damping fins. In short, we must accept that any powerboat will jump about unless she is used on very sheltered or inland waters.

The beginner's boat should be light in total weight so that when she hits a quay, another boat, or when she is being manhandled alongside a dock, she is within the capability of the owner to control. Naturally, weight is relative and it is surprising how easy it is in anything but a strong wind to manhandle a two, or even four ton boat. In general, the boat should be between 20 and 30 ft for easy manhandling. Of course, if she has to be hauled up and down on a trailer, then she wants to be much lighter. Even with a trailer winch, one or two people will not wish to deal with a boat much bigger than 22 ft except under ideal conditions. Even where the facilities are excellent a 28-footer is just about the limit, and this assumes exceptionally good mechanical handling equipment and trailer, a good hard or exceptional beach, protection from cross-winds, no swell and no big fast boats thundering past, throwing up a lumpy wash.

A beginner's boat also needs strength. This can only be achieved by careful workmanship and ample fastenings; massive components are not synonymous with strength. Though it is possible to build additional strength into a boat, it is not easy. In general one wants a boat which has initially been well built with adequate strength. Local weaknesses in deck or superstructure are not really important, since these can be stiffened.

Another quality which a powerboat needs is ruggedness. This is not quite the same as strength. It is an undefinable quality made up of half a million details. It is something which experienced owners appreciate, often without being able to put a finger on it. It includes a host of details, such as hand-rails which do not pull out, stanchions which are set slightly inboard so that they are not bent in whenever the boat rolls alongside another yacht. It embraces cleats which are bolted and not screwed, stern glands which have locking nuts on top of their fastening nuts, rigging and lifelines that start taut and stay that way, steering wires that can be grabbed hold of without coming away when the boat gives an unexpected lurch. Ruggedness is a highly desirable quality in any yacht, but it is *essential* in the beginner's boat.

Ruggedness certainly includes the ability to run aground with relative impunity. This requires a well protected propeller and rudder. There used to be a delightful craze for boats made with twin skegs, one either side of the propeller. The Dorset Lake Boatyard used to have a standard production series of these boats with rounded bows. The propeller was so well up that the tips of the blades were sufficiently far above the bottom of the skegs to give very real protection. As a result, these boats could be driven hard ashore on gravelly ground, with the engine going full belt. This is the ideal and, of course, one achieves it with most outboard engines since these tilt up when the skeg touches the ground.

Outboard engines also give extremely good manoeuvrability, since the whole engine and propeller turns when the helm is put over. This turns the boat sharply and is a great help under difficult situations. For instance, it is a big asset when trying to get away from a quay wall with an onshore wind.

My personal preference, for a beginner, would not be an outboard boat, since it tends to be heavy on fuel and maintenance costs; additionally, this type does not teach basic boat-handling and seamanship. However, this is not an overwhelming prejudice and for people who have to haul their boats up on trailers, or where the minimum initial price is an overwhelming factor, then a great deal is to be said for learning in an outboard boat.

With the current strong demand for fast boats, those capable of only six or eight knots are depressed in price often enough. This is a typical speed for a beginner. Additionally, this type of boat will have small running costs, often enough low maintenance expenses, coupled with a fairly high degree of safety and reliability. She is also less likely to be damaged if run aground, or hammered into a quay, and should be easier to handle, also more comfortable in a rough sea, as compared with a fast boat.

A type of launch which fits the bill rather well is often called a 'work-boat'. This is a reflection on its simple finish and the fact that it is often used by boatyards and contractors. The type does not seem to be much advertised in the yachting magazines and the indications are that they do not change hands all that often. It could well be that the only way to get one is to buy one new, or build one. It might be worth trying an advertisement in the 'Boats Wanted' column of the yachting magazines.

There are several firms which specialise in this type of boat so that when it comes to buying from them, one gets the value of series production. Such a firm will almost certainly have one of their boats afloat for demonstration runs. If you go to them in a slack period, which for most yards extends from about July to January, the chances are they would give you an extensive demonstration which amounts to half-a-day's tuition.

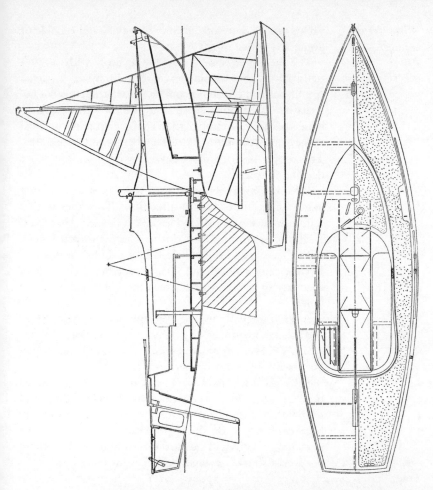

Designed by Oliver Lee of Burnham on Crouch, Essex, the N.23 class is a glassfibre racing boat. She is especially suitable for family day sailing as the forward end of the cockpit is covered by a cuddy. The fin ballast keel gives good stability, yet is easily removed for laying up in a confined space. Full internal buoyancy ensures that this yacht will float if flooded. Dimensions are: L.o.a. 23′ 3″. L.w.l. 19′ 2″. Beam 6′ 5″. Draught 3′ 8″. Displacement 1,900 lbs. Sail area 215 sq ft.

Naturally, everybody wants a seaworthy boat. But if ever there was a word hard to define it is 'seaworthy'. One might describe it as 'suitable for the local weather conditions and waters'. The plain fact is that very few yachts can be described as *fully seaworthy* and capable of going anywhere in any weather.

The beginner should go for a boat with a high standard of seaworthiness, bearing in mind his local conditions and cruising ground. Seaworthiness is largely a matter of proportion, so that one should stick fairly close to the recommendations in the graphs on ideal shapes. Another measure of seaworthiness is deck area. The more offshore the boat is to operate, the more decking she needs.

Most beginners will not want to go out for anything less than an hour's perambulation. This means that minimum accommodation at least is needed. However, a cabin costs money and this is where an open launch with a simple cuddy or shelter may well be the answer. Even a canvas hood and curtain can be made to give adequate shelter and space for a miniature galley and a toilet.

A hood virtually extends the area which is decked in, and hence improves the seaworthiness. For offshore work, or even exposed estuaries, a completely open boat is risky for a beginner.

As with sail, the beginner should first get 'web-footed'. Once he has learnt basic boat-handling and seamanship, picked up weather wisdom, and generally become at home on the sea, he can then go on to the next stage. This will be racing, cruising, water-skiing, deep-sea fishing, or whatever takes his fancy.

10 *Retired racing yachts*

Most young men and women, when looking for a sailing cruiser that is going to suit them, want something fast. The trouble is that fast boats are normally expensive, whereas young people are short of money. However these same people are generally prepared to tolerate a low standard of comfort. For them there is an interesting selection of retired racing boats which can be bought already converted, or unconverted, for cruising and passage racing. These boats are also suitable, in many cases, for day sailing, for pottering round with a young family (after certain modifications have been made) and for inshore handicap racing.

There used to be a lot of interest in old 6, 8 and 12 metres, fifteen and more years ago. But as these boats became rather long in the tooth, and plenty of other yachts became available, interest waned. Now it has revived, helped a little by the availability of a few 5·5 metre yachts suitable for conversion.

It must be admitted right away that this type of yacht, though fast, can be shockingly wet. I recall a race from Poole to Yarmouth. It was a close reach across Poole Bay and we filled our ex-6 metre '*Finetta*' with water up to the level of the settees, even though we were pumping pretty continuously. We wanted to win, and were driving hard, but still, it took us three-quarters of an hour pumping, after we got in, to clear her.

Also this kind of boat is cramped. The 'Sixes' used to be reckoned a bit tight, down below. But the 5·5 metre class are worse, and I have always felt that one (admittedly minor) reason this class never made solid progress was that they never commanded the same sort of second-hand price that 'Sixes' used to do, just after they finished their primary racing career.

On the other hand an old 'Eight' has lots of room below. The main snag here is that they are so long, from the tip of their thin elegant bow, to the far end of their infinite counters, that they cost a fortune to paint and to lay up for the winter. Twelve metres are just marvellous, in so many ways. They go so very fast in all weathers, have masses of room below, don't need an engine, go delightfully even with a tiny engine, have space for a big engine if you want, convert very easily to yawl, or more sensibly to a ketch and so on. But their snags match their assets. They are so big that few people can afford to run them, they are hard to find, at least in good condition, and hard to sell once you must finally part. But for sheer speed, elegance, grace, pace and space, not to say one-upmanship, there is nothing that comes near a 'Twelve'. They make those modern prestige boats, the crack ocean racers, look ugly, slow, contrived, rule-cheaters.

Getting back to a more generally practical level, there are plenty of out-classed Dragons about. At present they are available from £150 for a rather tired one, up to £1,000 and more. The number and condition of their sails naturally affects their price. If you find a Dragon with several suits of good sails, but only want to do a little racing, you can sometimes get back a little of the purchase price by selling off some of the sails. Dragons are very cramped indeed, down below. There is room for two pipe cots, a basic galley and a toilet bucket, but not much more. However with patience a lot can be done to convert a Dragon into a cruiser with reasonable room inside. It is the sort of thing a competent amateur shipwright could do, but if a yard does the work the cost would seldom be justified by the value of the final product.

To convert a Dragon to best advantage, it is advisable to make an entirely new cabin top. Carry it out to the

A motor-sailer intended especially for deep-sea cruising and fishing. This powerful yacht was designed by A. Mylne and Company of Royal Terrace, Glasgow, and she has a remarkable saloon with an effective length of almost 19'. This makes for comfortable living aboard. There are five berths, though the saloon settees could have backs made to hinge up so as for form two extra berths. Dimensions are: L.o.a. 36'. L.w.l. 33' 6". Beam 10' 6". Draught 3' 6".

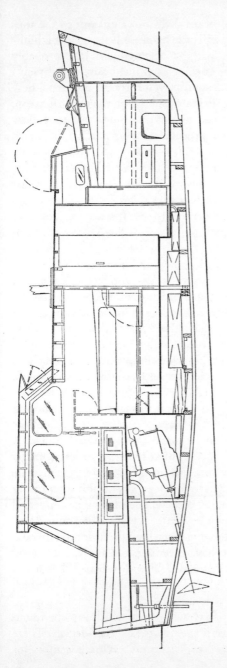
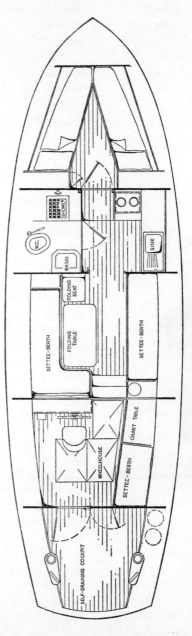

SHOWER

W.C.

BASIN

FOLDING SEAT

SINK

SETTEE - BERTH

FOLDING TABLE

SETTEE - BERTH

CHART TABLE

WHEELHOUSE

SETTEE - BERTH

SELF-DRAINING COCKPIT

inside face of the beam shelf, not right out to the top-sides. This arrangement gives the advantages of a built-up topsides boat without the ugliness. It is probably worth cutting the cockpit back one beam. For myself I would carry the cabin top well forward and step a new light alloy spar, with masthead rig, on the new cabin top.

Converting a 5·5 metre it would pay to follow roughly the same procedure. Above all it is worth having a professional plan drawn up. This not only saves mistakes, and hence money, while converting. More important it ensures that the finished boat has poise, appearance and finish, so that she is worth some-thing when the time comes to sell. It is also the best way to ensure the available space is used to maximum advantage.

It is worth comparing the price of this type and size of yacht with some of the mass-produced 2, 3 and 4 tonners available today. Plenty of people buy these, feeling that it makes sense to get a brand new, or almost new yacht. They feel, with reason, that one of these modern miniature cruisers will be cheap to maintain, is small enough to trail home behind a car, and is shallow enough to potter up little creeks. All this is true enough. Unfortunately a great many of these modern tiny cruisers are as slow as somnolent snails. They are boring to sail, useless often in passage racing, depreciate like cars, and too often lack the thoroughbred touch. A converted racing boat, costing the same or less initially, may cost more to run, but probably will not depreciate as fast. For the owner who does most of his own fitting out, the extra running costs will be small. The converted racing machine will be wetter when she is going faster, but no worse at the same speed than the little modern box. Most racing boats have breeding, and are built by good yards of the best material. I know I'm biased, but it is a bias based on solid experience. I dislike a boat which dares to try and bore me.

Another class of ex-racing boat which is to be found all round the coast is the out-classed half-decker. There have been racing classes in most yachting centres for years which come within the following broad category:

Overall length between 17 ft and 25 ft, two, three or four-man racing day-boat, usually three-quarter decked. With a fin keel often, sometimes with a centre-board as well or instead: normally with no cabin, or only a small cuddy which is sometimes portable. These boats are often particularly cheap if they have no cabin-top. They are usually very confined inside, and only suitable for two people, who preferably have to be young and extra enthusiastic.

At the larger end of the scale there are the out-classed ocean racers. These boats usually fetch useful prices as ordinary cruisers. However many people like the occasional offshore race, so that a boat which rates badly can sometimes be bought to advantage as she is unlikely to win even when lucky. Then again the change of fashion and the switch many owners are making to fibreglass means some of these dated offshore racers are hard to sell. The sharp-eyed buyer may be able to pick up an old ocean racer cheaper than a similar sized normal cruiser simply because the boat is so obviously a racing machine. She may well have a rather high mast, too little beam by current standards, a rather draughty-looking open-plan interior, and a general air of starkness. Buy her and modernise her, and you have a boat which can win in passage racing, give years of pleasant cruising, and is all the time faster and more fun than more stodgy cruisers.

A word of caution is due here. Avoid a very old racing boat, as she is likely to be a constant trial. Virtu-ally all racing boats are built lightly, heavily canvassed, and subject to a lot of hard driving. In their late middle age they start giving trouble, which increases apace. Unless you are one of those owners who enjoy extensive repair and renewal work (as plenty do), then get a boat with some years of life left in her. There is no reason why, subject to a sound backbone, you should not extensively replank and reframe a boat, before starting on the deck, chain plates and so on. The work is interest-ing and rewarding mentally, though seldom financially.

But if you primarily want to enjoy sailing rather than boatbuilding, get a sound boat.

'A sound boat' is a relative term, naturally. In an old racing boat it is usual and not worrying to find a sprinkling of cracked frames, say one in twelve. There will be evidence of hard thrashing to windward, with signs of movement at the beam ends. Indications of deck leaks are almost inevitable if the boat is more than ten years old. These defects need not worry you, and a surveyor will have no trouble in assessing whether the boat has been over-driven or is rotten unto death. Frames are not hard to double or renew, but the deck can be a problem. A laid deck (that is one made up of relatively narrow planks caulked and payed) is only effective if the wood is hard and the planking about an inch thick. Less than this and there is not the physical distance needed to take the caulking and paying, sufficient for a constantly water-tight join.

Racing boats have light deck planking since top weight is to be avoided. And for the same reason they seldom have decks thick enough to remain watertight. It would be bad enough if these boats were not driven by tall masts carrying clouds of sail. The wringing stress this puts up is seldom appreciated. It is tantamount, indeed is closely analagous, to putting the engine on a long stalk, twenty or so feet above the deck. Inevitably the boat is wrenched and tortured. So she leaks. This does not matter much in a boat used for an afternoon's sailing. It does matter on a cruiser.

One answer is to canvas the deck, but it is seldom a remedy. Besides the canvas rarely lasts more than six years, sometimes much less. Trakmark may be better, as it does not require painting and is likely to last longer. But the truth must be faced; to make a tight strong deck there is nothing like marine ply. This material cannot distort in its own plane, whereas the deck planks can and do move very slightly, each one in relation to its neighbour.

It can be argued that the ply panels may leak at their seams. Why have seams? Get the ply scarphed up in the factory in as long lengths as possible, so that there are only one or two joins in the whole length of the boat. The limitations in the lengths of the ply will be the size of ply sheets that can conveniently be handled. I find that with three people one can manage pieces up to 16 or 20 feet long but that 28 feet long is like trying to manhandle a boa-constrictor. (Not that my experience extends to these snakes; my imagination does, though.)

Pre-scarphing the ply before laying the deck is not all that difficult, but the factory will do it for you for about 20s. per scarph, and sand off the ply again, so it is sensible to have the work done in the plywood factory. Naturally only the best marine ply is used. Once laid, this sort of deck gives the boat a new lease of life. Not only does it stiffen the whole boat quite remarkably, it also stops those leaks which are usually the start of many of her troubles.

To lay the new deck it is necessary to take off all the fittings. But it is a brass farthing to a chancellor's budget that plenty of the fittings will anyhow need regalvanising or overhauling. So one makes a virtue of necessity and gets the fittings worked over at the same time as the new deck goes on. This is also a good opportunity to extend or reduce the size of the cockpit, move the mast, or maybe re-rig as a yawl or ketch for easier handling, and drop in an engine.

All this costs a lot of money, and it is likely that the work will have to be done in stages as far as possible. As to whether the boat is worth it, the broker and surveyor should be able to give you a good idea. At the present time it is seldom worth having this sort of extensive conversion done in a yard, but well worth doing it on an amateur basis, or part amateur, but with some professional help.

By 'worth it' I mean that the expenditure in a good quality yard will be too high when added to the first cost of the boat, in general, because the whole point of buying an ex-racing boat is to get a cheap fast cruiser, and for the money spent one would be better advised to buy a conventional cruiser which needs less work.

However each case must be balanced on its merits. One thing is certain; many many people who build themselves baby cruisers from kits or from scratch would give themselves less work, and end up with a better basic boat if they converted a good racing boat instead. They would also find the job shorter and so get in more sailing. Faster sailing too, though in some cases perhaps less comfortable cruising.

When it comes to the engine in a converted racing boat, there must inevitably be some conflicting thoughts and prejudices. For a start it is inevitable to feel that such a perfect, easily driven hull should not be sullied by an engine. The next thought is that we almost all have to be back in time for work, and children at school on Monday mornings. This means being back on moorings regardless of the calms, headwinds and foul tides. So an engine seems to be inevitable. What about an outboard over the side? Not so good, because they fall overboard, even when tied on, are not reliable and not easy to ship at sea. If they are fitted up with their own special locker, and some device like a hinged bracket which folds down over the yacht's side, or back into the deck locker, then some of the troubles are minimised.

But in the end most owners decide on an inboard. Should it be tiny, or in line with modern cruiser requirements and of ample horse-power? My own thoughts are that it should not be so large as to dominate the boat, but should be big enough to push the boat against the strongest local tides with a persistent light head wind blowing into the tall mast. That way the engine is a real friend when it is most needed. It adds a lot to the value of the boat and makes her not only worth more in the second-hand market, but also much easier to sell.

It would normally be sense to put a light, fairly fast-revving petrol engine into an ex-racing hull, as these engines give a good power-to-weight ratio. They also tend to be compact for their power and incidentally cheap. There is one small snag. For reliability it is best to go for a diesel, preferably one that can be hand-started.

A boat that is likely to have a lot of water inboard such as we are discussing is just the sort of boat that should *not* have an engine that depends on electrical current to make it function. So there is a case for the more expensive diesel engine. But one must avoid the bulky heavy type of diesel, as they take up too much of the limited amount of room, and are too heavy for their power.

Another aspect of this type of boat is the sail area and disposition. Racing boats carry a lot of sail, as a general rule. This gives fast exhilarating cruising, but it also means stressed hulls and sometimes over-stressed crews. There is a lot of sense in cutting a portion off the boom, or maybe reducing the mast height, or perhaps both. If the mast is doubtful, and new sails are needed, then the opportunity might be taken to re-rig, going for a masthead sail-plan and an alloy spar. But this is beginning to sound costly, so it is seldom worth doing unless new gear is needed anyway.

There are several morals to be drawn from all this. When looking at an ex-racing boat, it is going to be important not only to look at the hull, but also the amount of conversion work that has already been done. Has it been well done, to a plan drawn by a competent designer? If an engine is fitted then that is a job saved, provided the installation is satisfactory. This is an instance, like so many, where it is worth making a written list of pros and cons, and seeing how they add up.

It will be seen from all this that in this field of boat-buying, there are wide and by no means obvious opportunities. The kind of man who dabbles in this type of boat-buying may be compared to the take-over tycoon. Not because the boatbuyer is necessarily well equipped financially, but because he sees assets where others fail to notice anything unusual.

To give an example which might tantalise a few people. On the Clyde there has been built up a very fine class of 8 metre Cruiser–Racers to the new Cruiser–Racer rule. As the years go by the older boats become outclassed by the latest additions to the fleet. One result is that the older boats sell at a price which is considered to be their current value as plain fast cruisers. This is fair enough, because they are indeed delightful cruisers. But as a student of yachting history I can safely predict that one summer there will be a bit of a sensation. Sooner or later someone is going to buy one of these outclassed boats. He will either be a fine helmsman, or a keen owner who is happy to turn the helm over to a top-class helmsman. He will gather together a crew who are keen, experienced, and tough. They'll gut the boat, probably do something moderately radical about the rig, possibly throw out the engine, or at least change it, and *tune*. Above all they'll tune. And then they'll go on to have a highly successful season. They'll not necessarily clean the board, but they will shake the new boats considerably. This has happened in other classes often enough, and it tends to happen to almost every restricted class once in a while.

This is the sort of opportunity which occasionally turns up in all sorts of racing fleets, from racing dinghies to offshore racers.

11   *An old, old boat*

As a general rule, yachts last 50 years. However, there are still a few well-built wooden yachts going afloat every season after 75 years. Conversely, steel yachts don't seem to last the full 50 years; iron ones do, though these are extremely rare and are usually over 70 ft with clipper bows and an air of early Victorian opulence.

Undecked boats tend to survive no more than 40 years because they can 'work' and flex more easily. One very seldom meets a plywood boat that can boast more than 40 summers, but this may be because the plywood manufacturers in those days were not able to cope with marine conditions.

So, as a basis, let us say that an old boat is one that is somewhere over 35 years old, or possibly less, if she has led an energetic racing life under a series of hard-driving owners.

Such a boat is a good buy for a certain type of owner and a thoroughly bad buy for everyone else. This special type of owner gets more fun out of working on his boat than he does from the sailing. The type is very common all over the world. I remember a retired professional man on the East Coast, universally known as 'Allah's brother Alf'. 'Allah's brother' lived on an East Coast river where he kept his converted fishing boat. He worked on her from the second week in July right through the year to the first week of the next July. Then he put to sea for one glorious week, straight out into the North Sea for $3\frac{1}{2}$ days, hard-over-with-the-helm and straight back again. Thus it was every year, never more or less than one week's sailing and 51 weeks pottering on board. He always seemed perfectly happy and his boat undoubtedly was a success because it gave him what he wanted – endless fun.

For anybody intending to do serious offshore work, it is a mistake to go for a very old boat. There are, of course, yachts 40 and more years of age that will pass a very stringent survey, but such boats will never seem their age and the chances are that some sellers will conceal the age of the boat (if they can). This type of boat will almost always have had continuous expensive maintenance in a first-class yard and this is the sort of boat which will last up to 70 years or more. (It is worth noting that even a very well built boat, annually maintained to the highest standard will not necessarily see her 70th summer, particularly if she was rather lightly built in any one aspect, or given a big power plant. In this connection, of course, power may be from the sails or engine, as the racking stresses of either will be just as destructive.)

The owner who intends to do no more than normal coastal summer cruising can get a great deal of fun out of a really old boat, with the added satisfaction that she will almost certainly be beautiful and characterful. Ugly boats do not get the loving care and attention needed to keep a boat going year after year.

When buying a boat of this type, it is essential to resist inevitable temptations. Perhaps she has no electric light aboard, no echo-sounder, no anchor winch. Before putting this equipment aboard, spend time and money on new garboard planks. Put up with inadequate galley stowage but not with inadequate rudder pintles.

The chances are that the rig will be old-fashioned. Put up with this for at least a season. The boat may go extremely well under her dated rig and, in any case, a season's use under the existing sail plan will show how much weather helm she carries, whether she is over-canvassed and, most important of all, whether she is worth spending money on.

Re-rigging can often be done inexpensively, particularly if the sail plan alterations are carefully designed. There is no reason why a competent amateur should not do much of the work, if not all of it. The more modern the rig, the less total sail area for a given amount of drive. This is just what is required, for these old hulls should not be loaded with an increase in sail area.

By the same token careful re-engining may be worth-while, but too much power will shake up and over-drive the weakening hull. By all means put 12 h.p. into a 6-tonner, but don't put in 40, as is sometimes seen in new designs.

Occasionally there is a temptation to buy a really old boat for her lead. A 25 ft w.l. boat may well have 2½ tons of lead in her keel and often enough the quoted price of lead will be, perhaps, £110 per ton. If somebody offers a 25 ft w.l. boat for only £400, under these conditions it looks as if the boat is virtually being given away, since there appears to be £275 worth of lead on her. How-ever, the quoted price of lead is not the same as that which a scrap merchant will give. There is also the very real cost of getting the lead off the boat and then there is the cost of the replacement iron keel, or the disposal of the hull. So, in general, it seldom pays to buy solely because of the lead.

Having said all this, it is inevitable that next week someone will buy a 60-year-old boat and win an im-portant race with her, or maybe cruise safely twice round the world without a moment's bother. The trouble with basic principles is that there is always some efficient yachtsman whose skill and luck appear to make nonsense of primary rules. However, there are also the people who don't come back to tell the tale!

Certainly, 15 years ago it was possible to have a great deal of success by buying a really old boat, modernising her quite extensively and then racing her. But com-petition now is much tougher and the chances of success are really rather slim.

12 *What affects value*

Two almost identical yachts may come on the market at the same time, and the asking price of one may be double the other. A newcomer to the sport may think this is completely illogical; the two boats may look almost the same. They may indeed have the same value of materials and workmanship in them, but there can still be a heavy price differential.

The name of the designer and the builder are big influences. It is reasonably considered that famous designers only produce top quality boats of good shape and specification. On the whole this is true, though any experienced owner can recall the name of a boat or three which is frankly a poor buy, yet she comes from the board of a famous designer. One reason for this is that designers do not leap straight from school to the top of the design tree. In their early years they sometimes produce boats which they would like to forget about later. Occasionally too the reverse process takes place. A designer gets old, tired, spends less and less time afloat. He depends on his assistants, and even leaves important drawings to third-year apprentices. The resulting boats are less than wonderful, though it is mercifully rare that they are actually third-rate.

With builders there are the same human problems. Builders cannot gather together in the first years a core of skilled shipwrights, a blacksmith, interior joiner, mechanic and rigger. It is usually a generation before a yard can turn out the sort of boat that causes extensive deep-seated envy. That subtle aura, compounded usually of very deep gloss varnish, a complete absence of any visible fastenings, no noticable straight line nor yet any too obvious curve anywhere in the hull, takes a lot of time, skill and patience to produce.

To accentuate this point, I have surveyed and examined yachts built on both sides of the Atlantic, on both sides of the North Sea, on both sides of the English Channel, on both sides of the Irish Sea, on both sides of Hadrians Wall. After all this I am certain that one yard stands out at present just ahead, but quite firmly ahead of all others. It is capable of building yachts which match the finest that have been produced in all the years back to the beginning of the century. In short, it can, when an owner wants and is prepared to pay, achieve that sort of breathless loveliness which I find beyond words.

It so happens, however, that I once surveyed a yacht built about twenty-five years ago by this company. It was reasonably sound, seaworthy enough, the scantlings were not skimped. But it was far, very far from that pinnacle of workmanship which they can now achieve. I have learned since the survey that when this boat was built the yard were just beginning to climb to the heights. I suspect too that they did not put their best shipwrights on the job.

So though the market is right to put a premium on boats with good parentage, one must take a long hard look at the boat and not take the birth certificate on trust. I must admit that I cannot recall a yacht which was both designed by a top name, and shaped by a top yard that was not at least reasonably good.

A more dubious asset is the phrase 'Famous owner' on a broker's circular. Some people by virtue of their racing successes or prowess at cruising can and do expect to sell their boats at above the market price. Here it is worth treading warily. There are quite a few owners whose boats I would strongly recommend, simply because these owners are thoroughly experienced and treat their boats well. They do not stint money on the upkeep, avoid running onto rocky lee shores, always lay up under cover. They neither fit, nor allow yards to fit such unpleasant but initially hard-to-notice things as brass hinges with steel pins. They care for their yachts thoroughly. These boats are desirable buys.

But there are other owners who are just as famous, but who should not be followed. One in particular comes to mind, a well-known racing skipper. He wins

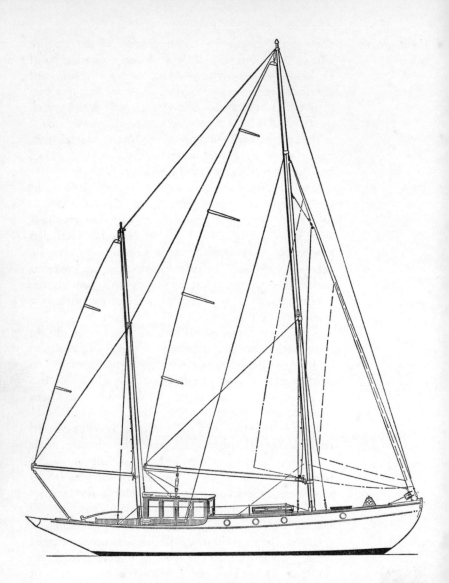

Amid all the clamour of modern advertising, it is easy to forget that an older boat can be better value than a new one. Most boats can be modernised, and this will transform not only their appearance but often their performance. 'Judith' ex-'Rowan II' owned by David Donald is a good example. A particularly interesting detail of her alteration is the addition of a bowsprit, since it is much more usual to remove rather than add this type of spar. But every case of modernisation has to be treated on its merits.

races by sheer hard driving of the most relentless kind. There is nothing wrong in this, in fact it is the only way to win and go on winning. But he tends to buy lightly built boats, craft which in practice can only stand a limited amount of flogging round stiff courses. I recall going over one. She showed signs of hard usage from bow pulpit (with its various dents and bends) to the stern 'pushpit', with its forward foot still showing signs of uprooting where I would guess that a spinnaker sheet had caught with a jolt. From masthead, with its gouges where the spinnaker halliard had chaffed, to heel of keel, where she must have gone aground while travelling at a fair pace, judging by the grooving of the lead. She was basically a good boat, otherwise that owner would never have bought her, nor had so much success. But whether she was worth buying after he had finished with her was quite another matter.

There is the obvious consideration too that no successful racing owner will sell his boat while she still has the potential to stay at the top of the fleet. So though there is sense in buying a boat with a lot of flags to her name, it is worth tempering one's enthusiasm when the bidding is in progress.

A surprising difference to a boat's price is made by her location. It is surprising because it is often out of proportion to the cost of moving her. I recall a half-decker for sale for £100 in Blyth when her sisterships where offered at £220 and more on the South Coast and on the Clyde. The cost of moving this boat to either of these centres was at that time about £50 including loading, off-loading and insurance.

Generally speaking the Solent, and especially the Hamble, commands the highest price. In fact Cowes, because it involves a time-consuming journey across the water, is not quite such a good place to sell a boat as the Hamble. In Scotland a similar situation arises. A boat is easiest sold if she is on the Gareloch, in Dumbarton, or actually in Glasgow. The further away, the fewer people will take the trouble to inspect her, so the lower must go her price before she does sell.

Parallel situations arise in other yachting areas, and yachting countries. This means that there are some places where boats are 25% cheaper, and occasionally 60% cheaper than identical boats in fashionable or accessible locations. One surprising thing about price reductions is that they are not logical. For instance Essex is nearer London than the Hamble, well served by road and rail, and has ample yachting facilities. Yet for a long time boats at Burnham-on-Crouch were markedly cheaper than those on the Hamble and at other yachting centres on the South Coast.

A yacht's class affects her price in several ways. If she is one of an Olympic class, then the price will tend to hold up. But if that class gets dropped from the Olympics, the class average price will take a beating. If the class is active and growing this can put something like 5% or 10% onto the value. If it is a class which is fading the reverse applies. If the class is being actively superseded, then the price can be in the bargain basement.

The sort of situation that occasionally crops up is this: A club has a fleet of fifteen 18-ft dinghies, a one-design. For years they have given grand racing, and they probably exactly fit the local waters. Then gradually one owner concentrates on tuning his boat and himself, so that he dominates the class. The others get discouraged. Or maybe the boats are just plain old and beginning to get a tiny bit flimsy, though far from unseaworthy for the job. Or maybe the boats are well enough matched among themselves, but all the neighbouring clubs go over to racing planing dinghies or catamarans. These flyers make the traditional boats look pretty slow. Whatever the cause, sometimes a whole class, all in one area, comes on the market. Or maybe it is only five boats out of the fifteen. Whatever the number, if it is more than two or three, the price may be really low. For a start the owners will all be dying to get into a new fast class. Then most of the boats will have stopped depreciating due to their age. On top of this the owners will be competing among themselves to find the all too few buyers.

Is this a true chance to pick up a bargain? For a start a lot depends on the sort of boat we are talking about. Some of these dying racing classes are just exhausted. The fastenings between frames and planking are stretched, all the centre-line backbone bolts have corroded away, the planking is soft and soggy. Better to keep clear; this is just a load of trouble.

But sometimes the class which is dying out in one locality is thoroughly active in a nearby centre. The price is low only in the one town, and ten or fifteen per cent higher in the next county. This is one reason why a buyer gains by going to a broker. He will know about these local differences, if he is worth his commission.

13 *Equipment influences the price*

Two yachts, seen afloat on moorings from a distance of fifty yards may look alike. The owner of one is asking £2,000, and he gets it. The owner of the other is asking £1,200 and cannot find a buyer. The boats are from the same "stable", the same age, and have won the same load of silverware. It is only when you go aboard that you notice the difference between the two yachts. One has small, direct-acting sheet winches and no halliard winches, the other has three winches round the mast base and geared sheet winches. One has a diesel engine, the other a petrol unit, and so on.

Equipment on a boat affects the price in odd ways. This is because it can be divided into classes roughly as follows:

1. Items which plainly enhance a boat's value, usually by making her easier to sail, or faster. (They are on the verge of being considered essential.) Roller reefing is a fair example of this.
2. Items which are most attractive, often useful, but far from essential, and more in the category of luxuries. An example would be a searchlight on a 36-ft motor-cruiser.
3. Items which are fashionable but not necessarily an all-round asset. For instance, plenty of sailing cruisers around 10 tons are coming out with wheel steering. It costs a lot, needs maintenance, and sometimes breaks down. Against this, it can take the sting out of steering a weather-helmy boat, also it often makes for more room in the cockpit, and it can help a lot when the helmsman wants to steer from leeward.
4. Items which are not essential, but whose absence gives the boat a feeling of being 'skinned out' for racing, or built down to a rock-bottom price. The absence of this sort of equipment depresses a boat's

price noticeably; buyers seem to feel that they are looking at an incomplete boat. One example might be a pump toilet on a 4 tonner. After all, a bucket toilet is light, hygienic, does not break down, cannot endanger the boat through leaks at the skin fittings, and saves a lot of weight. But these days everyone expects a pump toilet in virtually any boat with a cabin.

5. Items which are essential. The obvious example is a dinghy with a cruiser. If the cruiser is offered for sale without a dinghy, then a buyer must allow at least an extra £20, and more like £45, or even £85, for a dinghy, even for quite a small cruiser.

For every buyer, the equipment will have a different significance. The man who sails single-handed will almost certainly want an echo-sounder on a boat over 5 tons, and probably be keen to have one even on a 2-tonner. But the father of two hardy teenagers, sailing on a shoal draft 4-tonner is perhaps hard up paying school fees. For him, a lead and line will give the boys something to do, teach them a valuable skill as well as keep them amused, and save between £30 and £60 or more, according to the quality of the instrument.

Fashion also has a strong influence in this whole matter. For instance everyone buying a motor-cruiser wants a twin-screw diesel boat. This is regardless of the fact that modern diesels make a horrible noise, and their scream is remarkably hard to suppress, even with a big expenditure on soundproofing. In five or fifteen years' time, diesels may be right out of fashion, and the demand may switch to Wankel engines, gas turbines, or maybe back to petrol-paraffin units if only someone spends enough money on advertising them. One obvious conclusion from all this is that a buyer short of money should avoid the fashionable, concentrate on what is to him essential and, at the same time, not be biased by equipment which is no real asset. The clever thing to do is to take a sheet of paper and write down each item of gear absent, add up the cost of buying it *and* fitting

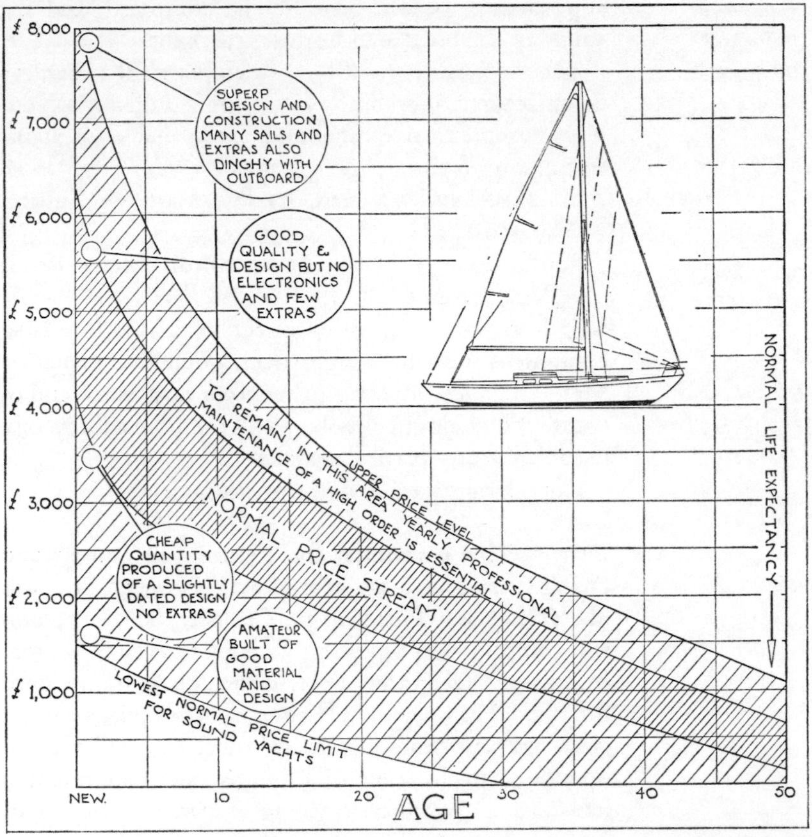
£ 8,000
£ 7,000
£ 6,000
£ 5,000
£ 4,000
£ 3,000
£ 2,000
£ 1,000
SUPERP DESIGN AND CONSTRUCTION MANY SAILS AND EXTRAS ALSO DINGHY WITH OUTBOARD
GOOD QUALITY & DESIGN BUT NO ELECTRONICS AND FEW EXTRAS
CHEAP QUANTITY PRODUCED OF A SLIGHTLY DATED DESIGN NO EXTRAS
AMATEUR BUILT OF GOOD MATERIAL AND DESIGN
TO REMAIN IN THIS AREA YEARLY PROFESSIONAL MAINTENANCE OF A HIGH ORDER IS ESSENTIAL
UPPER PRICE LEVEL
NORMAL PRICE STREAM
LOWEST NORMAL PRICE LIMIT FOR SOUND YACHTS
NORMAL LIFE EXPECTANCY
NEW.
10
20
30
40
50
AGE

A graph showing approximate prices of auxiliary Bermudan sloops between about 32′ and 36′ overall. This shows the diversity of prices, influenced by the initial quality of the design, workmanship and equipment. It indicates the rate of depreciation, shows where a bargain occurs, and points the importance of good annual maintenance. The price streams have to be wide to take into account convenient or remote location of yachts, current fashions, racing record, the type of engine installed, and all the other factors which affect a yacht's market value.

it, so as to see how much more money will be needed after the boat has been bought. On another sheet of paper make a separate list of gear aboard which enhances the value of the boat, and so makes her easier to sell in due course. When viewing other boats later, the lists appertaining to each boat can be compared, and the values of the boats seen in their true light.

When assessing the value of equipment it is hard to do an accurate job without a catalogue in front of you. Very comprehensive catalogues are available for about ten shillings from:

Simpson–Lawrence Ltd, 11 St Andrew's Square, Glasgow, C1.

South Western Marine Factors Ltd, Pottery Road, Poole, Dorset.

(Neither of these firms sell direct to private buyers so equipment must be bought from your local chandler. Many chandlers advertise in yachting magazines, and of course the catalogue suppliers will send the address of a chandler in any particular area.)

Considering specific items of equipment:

Dinghy. This is essential for virtually all cruisers and racing boats which are kept afloat. However, at places like Cultra and Burnham-on-Crouch, the yacht clubs run continuous comprehensive launch services, so that owners of keeled racing boats at such places do not need dinghies. The value of a dinghy depends on its length, type, age and condition. Many surveyors will give an opinion as to the value of a dinghy, and may mention its likely life expectancy. A big tender, say over 11 ft, may be cheaper second-hand than an 8-footer because the smaller size is more in demand. Rubber dinghies are becoming very popular, but it is worth remembering that they have a shorter life than most 'solid' models. They normally have to be sent back to the manufacturers for repair and this costs very nearly as much in transport as in labour. Most owners can repair most rigid type dinghies. Rubber boats need virtually no maintenance, they make far better life-rafts than 'solid' dinghies, and they do not chip the paint off their parent yacht's topsides, but they are hard to row.

Ply dinghies are cheap, easy to repair, never look anything more than what they are, but they are light in weight. Fibreglass dinghies do not stand up to continuous hard usage, and in practice appear to have a life expectancy of around 8 to 12 years in spite of advertising to the contrary. The better ones will far outlast the shoddy versions, also a lot depends on how they are made and treated. Light alloy dinghies stand a lot of rough usage, but are costly to repair. They are not so easy to maintain smartly, as for example they must be painted in accordance with a strict procedure, otherwise the paint chips off too easily.

Clinker dinghies are less frequently seen than formerly, partly because their initial cost is high, partly because they require skill to build, and this is a dying art. But they take a lot of punishment, will last 40 years or more, even if maltreated, and they look 'yachty'. However, they are heavy, costly to maintain, in that varnishing is awkward, and yet for their failings, they hold a place of strong affection in many yachtsmen's hearts.

When looking at a yacht's tender, see if it has a lot of internal buoyancy, enough to support the boat and four people, if the boat is 8 ft long, enough to support seven if it is 10 ft long. This means that at least all the space under all the thwarts should be solid with buoyancy material. This is because most of the fatal accidents in yachting are caused by capsizing dinghies. Another thing: Imagine what will happen if the dinghy does fill while fully laden. How will everyone hold on? Are there grab rails, or lifeline loops like those round a lifeboat, or maybe carrying handles. It is worth remembering the story of the dinghy that capsized in Loch Lomond. The crew of two were in the icy water for $2\frac{1}{2}$ hours before being picked up. During this time the boat was upside-down and the only thing they had to hold on to was *one* rudder gudgeon. They must have had very sore thumbs, clinging precariously to such a tiny morsel of metal so long.

Some boats are offered for sale with two dinghies. This is a real asset, particularly where the parent boat can only carry a very small dinghy. I have for some years carried a light, buoyant, but not very tough dinghy on the foredeck. For getting to and from the boat I use what we call the 'working dinghy'. This is a boat that is as big as we can drag up the shore, and too big to haul aboard the yacht. We leave it on moorings all weekend. It is larger and roomier, safer and easier to row than the biggest dinghy we could possibly heave aboard. In rough weather when going afloat it is a tremendous comfort, with its reserve of freeboard and buoyancy.

Outboard-motor. Linked with the yacht's dinghy is the 'outboard'. A second-hand outboard that has not been looked after has a very low value, and even one that has been well maintained is not worth much unless it is one of those powerful jobs, over 12 h.p. If the parent yacht is to be moored in a strong tide, then an outboard is important, and an unreliable one not to be tolerated. As a rough guide, a second-hand outboard between 1 and 5 h.p. might be assessed at its full value if virtually new, and assumed to lose about a quarter of its value each year. As every year passes, a bigger percentage of owners get outboards and it looks as if they will cease to be extras or luxuries in about 10 years' time.

Inflatable liferafts. Larger yachts must now by law have inflatable liferafts, as must yachts racing under RORC and CCA Rules, also under some local Club Rules.

Electronic gear. Equipment of this nature is now becoming increasingly fashionable, comprehensive, and beginning to form a significant portion of the value of all yachts down to 15 tons. For some equipment one might say, down to 6 tons.

Making a careful guess, I would say: An echo-sounder is fitted on most cruisers over 10 tons and half of those down to 5 tons. It is a fairly reliable long-lasting instrument, almost universally wanted. When assessing the value of an echo-meter remember it takes a little time to instal, so allow say £5 for this work on a small boat, and double on a larger one of over 12 tons.

Though radio-telephones are getting popular, they are by no means in general demand. Partly this is because owners go to sea to get away from the phone. This instrument seems to depreciate fast. One three years old is often valued at half its new price. Installation costs are significant and the standard of reliability seems to be relatively low, as compared with other electronic equipment on yachts.

An ordinary radio, with the usual direction-finder as used on all types of yachts, requires little installation and is in very general demand. Because it is easy to move this item from boat to boat, sellers tend to hang on to their radio and offer the yacht for sale without it. Current standards of reliability are fairly high, but when assessing second-hand value it is usual to assume that for a radio between three and five years old about half the new price should be taken. Older than this the value drops fast.

There is a growing demand for instrumentation, on power yachts and, particularly, on racing sailing yachts. On a 20-tonner it is entirely feasible that there may be £800 worth of electronic gear, taking the new cost. This will include a costly speedometer and a second simpler one as a cross-check in case the first gets seaweed round its rotator. There will be wind direction and speed indicators, two sets of direction-finding equipment, two echo-sounders and so on. When assessing this gadgetry, it is worth remembering that it needs maintenance, has a relatively limited life when compared with the basic yacht, and is more or less vulnerable, so it should be considered attractive for a cruising man, but should not be given too much weight. For serious racing it is essential, and so this gives the value a very different bias, according to the buyer's future intentions.

Winches. Sheet winches are almost universally fitted on all sailing cruisers of 5 tons and over, often found on 3-tonners and can be an asset on the very smallest cruiser. Very many yachts are 'under-winched'. Taking the broad view it is not far short of the full truth to say that only yachts designed for offshore racing, as well as a few pure cruisers (built mainly in the last twelve years) are properly equipped with sheet winches. On virtually every boat over 8 tons it is essential to have geared winches to give adequate power in all circumstances.

Geared winches cost a great deal of money, between £35 and £350, or even more, each. As a result, on big boats the total winch costs can run to thousands.

Many yachts, especially those built up to about 1950 have good, ungeared winches, usually with drum diameters below $3\frac{1}{2}$ inches. The winches are fine in moderate winds, but were fitted before the current practice of carrying genoas to windward in force 6. Under these conditions they are very poor. If this sort of winch is fitted, then it means replacements are likely to be needed, and to the cost of the winches must be added the cost of the bases and the labour of fitting. Even for cruising the ungeared winch is not satisfactory for boats over 10 tons.

It is rare for cheap boats to be properly equipped with winches. If buying a new series-built yacht, almost regardless of the builder or designer, I would order the boat without winches, and fit at least one size and probably two sizes bigger than the class normally have. One of the reasons why older boats are 'under-winched' is that they were built before the advent of terylene sails. In those days too much power would result in deformed sails and broken sheets.

Halliard winches present quite a different problem. They are desirable, and generally fitted on cruisers and racing boats over 10 tons. But they are heavy, often with their weight high up, so that for boats less than 24 ft on the waterline a case may be made for having tackles instead.

There is less tendency to under-winch for the halliards as the force required is normally not as big as that needed for sheeting home a headsail. If a boat has no halliard winches, and has got an alloy mast it may not be too easy to fit a winch to the spar, although a fully equipped yacht yard can manage. In this instance the winch will probably have to be fitted to the cabin top and a snatch block fitted at the mast base to lead the halliard horizontally to the winch. In addition, there may be cases where the cabin top requires stiffening, which will cost money.

Halliard winches come in two basic types: the reel kind which winds up an all-wire halliard as the sail is hoisted; and the type which looks like a top action sheet winch. This is used just to tighten the sail luff, after the sail has been hoisted most of the way up by hand. This second kind tends to be cheaper and to my mind much to be preferred. The other kind is slow, but worse, it tends to jam by crossing the wires as they are given that final tightening. True enough, this dangerous habit can be cured by introducing a piece of soft leather under the last few turns of wire, so preventing the wire bedding down too deeply as it tightens. But I, for one, have no wish to fiddle with pieces of leather, as we thunder round the lee mark in a welter of spray and closeby rivals, all in the middle of a dark draughty night.

Studying a yacht's gear, while assessing it from your own point of view, a lot can be learned about the boat. If she has a power bilge pump and a well-worn hand pump, then she probably leaks. If she has two compasses, then she has been owned by someone who really goes cruising, unless he happens to be a navigating enthusiast. Either way, he is probably knowledgeable and likely to look after his boat. A full set of lifejackets and complete safety equipment is a rare find in the boat's store. This man has either been frightened, or he keeps his boat well, or he has all this stuff because the offshore racing rules require it.

When examining gear in a store or on a boat, add up its value and divide the list in two: one column should show the essential items, the other show luxuries. Make up a third list of equipment which is missing. This is a great help in assessing what to bid for a boat.

14 *The strings and things*

Comparatively speaking, rigging is cheap. On inspection, a boat may be found to need a complete new set of rigging, but this will only cost between one and three per cent of the purchase price. For this reason, dud rigging should not be allowed to condemn a boat. Of course, it may indicate that the boat has not been well looked after. A man who neglects his rigging is skimping. What is worse, he is taking a risk with the main motive power, if the boat is sail-driven. The indications are that he is a bit of a fool, for a dismasting is not funny. Off a lee shore even a parting jib sheet can lead to a lot of trouble.

If galvanised wire rigging is showing faint traces of rust on it, then it is probably good for another season. To be on the safe side the shrouds can usually be turned end-for-end since it is the bottom end which goes first. In a few cases the wires may have special end terminals which do not permit this end-for-ending.

Just occasionally the red-brown wire rigging seems quite bright if rubbed. This indicates that the wire is stainless and what at first glance seemed to be rust is the oil oozing out of the wire, with discolouring which so-called stainless sometimes has.

If the wire is truly rusted, it should be renewed without hesitation. In view of the low price of wire the rule must be 'if in doubt—renew'. The forestay, in particular, should always be treated with the utmost pessimism. This is because it is so very important. If it breaks the mast could pivot down on the centreline of the ship, prevented from going to port or starboard by the shrouds. If it crashes into the cockpit, the crew could be seriously hurt. The forestay tends to have its galvanizing rubbed off it by the jib hanks and, of course, it cannot be made of that plastic-covered galvanised wire (which will last longer by virtue of this plastic cover) because the jib hanks will not run smoothly over the plastic.

If a boat is found to have stainless steel rigging the indications are that the owner has looked after her well, since this material costs about six times as much as ordinary galvanized wire. There is a good deal of doubt as to whether the extra cost is worth while, because there have been too many instances of stainless wire parting, and it does not give warning as galvanized wire does.

Galvanized wire seems to be the best for all-round use in temperate climates and generally lasts between 3–8 years, depending on the amount of care it gets and the number of miles sailed. Occasionally, it is found to last more than 16 years with really careful laying up and the elaborate use of preservatives (but not paint) when fitting-out.

Rigging renewal, like sail repairs and engine maintenance, is all part of the annual overhaul which every yacht needs. This is another reason why defective rigging should not deter a potential buyer. As a *very* rough rule indeed, an owner must expect to spend about £1 per ton TM on his rigging renewal and repair each year, if he goes in for normal summer cruising. For long range cruising, this figure will, of course, be at least doubled. For racing it must again be doubled and doubled again, according to the determination, enthusiasm and wealth of the owner. This approximate figure covers running and standing rigging.

A boat is rarely too lightly rigged if she is a cruiser. If anything, there is a tendency in Britain to overdo the thickness of the wire, except in small mass-produced cruisers which often have under-sized wires and grossly under-sized sheets in order to keep down the price. Naturally, racing boats tend to have fairly light rigging, but even here if one is buying a racing boat for racing the chances are the rigging will be the right thickness. If in doubt, just compare it with the rigging on several other boats of the same class.

Possibly the only time when rigging sizes will almost

The strings and things

certainly have to be thickened up is when buying a Dragon or 5·5 metre, or other racing boat to convert to a cruiser.

One of the reasons why rigging should not add much to the cost of buying a boat is that the components can be made up by an amateur. Splicing is not hard to learn and, in any case, Norseman terminals (from Norseman Ropes of Manningtree, Essex) can be used to avoid splicing. Using these terminals it is often possible to reduce the rigging diameter by one size, if the wires are changed from the traditional 7 × 7 (or 6 × 7) to 1 × 19 construction. *

In practice, the owner need worry a great deal less about his rigging wires than about the fittings at each end of them. Provided wire is not allowed to rust or, in the case of stainless steel, allowed to be fatigued, and provided it is not kinked, then it is very unlikely to break.

Rigging failures generally occur at the shackles and, occasionally, at the rigging screws. For this reason a $\frac{3}{8}''$ rigging screw should be used on a $\frac{1}{4}''$ dia. wire: indeed, it is not being over-cautious to use a $\frac{7}{16}''$ screw on a $\frac{1}{4}''$ wire, particularly if you will be sailing a lot far offshore.

It is well worth buying tested shackles and rigging screws and, of course, reducing the number of components as much as possible.

When looking over a boat's gear, if she has any 'natural' fibre ropes then these should be completely discounted, in almost every instance. Modern synthetics, such as Terylene, Ulstron and Courline; have completely superseded Manilla, Hemp and Sisal. The modern ropes are so much more pliable, a great deal stronger and last very much longer so that there is no reason at all for sticking to the older types of 'natural' ropes.

In the same way, modern Tufnol blocks last a very long time with virtually no maintenance. Under normal

---

* 7 × 7 means seven individual wires twisted into a 7-strand wire, and seven such wires twisted together to form the final rope.

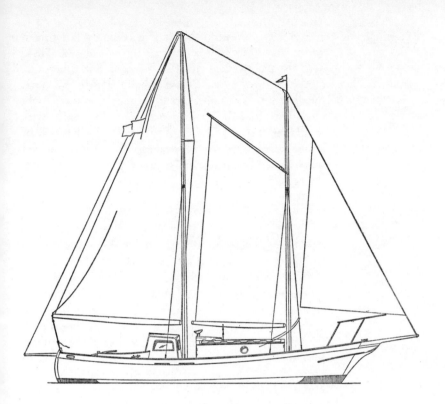

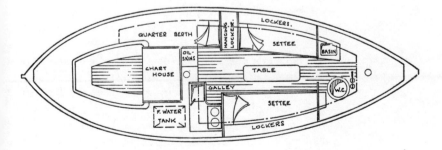

A well-designed boat of character is always a pleasure to own. It will hold its value better than many mass-produced conventional yacht, though it may not sell so quickly when the time comes to change. This 24ft Sharpie Schooner is easy to build, easy to sail, and has a modest draft which makes her suitable for estuary cruising. She was designed by Maitland Murray of Morris and Lorimers, Sandbank, Argyll.

cruising use, a Tufnol block will certainly last fifteen years. The same may be said for rigging screws. These need replacing if they are bent or rusting but, otherwise, can be expected to last a third or half the life of the boat. Incidentally, when inspecting rigging it is extremely important to handle the wires carefully. Each wire should be found made up into a neat labelled coil of large diameter to prevent kinking. It can be inspected when coiled but if for any reason it has to be laid out, the procedure is as follows:

Cut the lashings, stand the coil on edge and unroll it along the floor.

Any other procedure will almost certainly cause a kink and make the wire entirely valueless.

One problem with the new synthetic ropes is that they have trade names and these vary from country to country. On top of this, they are being developed each year with new types and characteristics coming out all the time. For anyone who is bemused by this proliferation, there is an easy and sensible way out: just write to Norseman Ropes Ltd, or Marlow Ropes Ltd, of Marlow House, Lloyd's Avenue, London, EC3, or Healey Brothers Ltd, of Cartridge Ropery, Heywood, Lancashire, or any other reputable maker, for their current catalogue. These not only list the latest products, but also indicate the best size and type for each individual job.

The actual rigging plan of a boat often dates her, sometimes quite accurately. For instance, very few cruisers have been built with runners in the last ten years. Older boats tend to have more rigging and therefore, cost more to maintain above deck. Modernisation here pays a double dividend, giving better performance and lower running costs. The cost of bringing a rigging plan up to date is nearly always worth while, provided the mast (or masts) do not have to be moved and not too many sails are needed. The science of rigging is changing all the time but the actual cost, as compared with the rest of the boat, is not going up.

15   *How the engine affects the value*

Just occasionally, when looking for a motor cruiser one will be found in which the machinery is worth more than the rest of the boat put together. Indeed, this situation occasionally occurs even with auxiliary cruisers. It usually happens when a new engine is put into an ageing boat.

From this it will be seen that the engine, or engines, can have a very strong influence on the asking price of a second-hand yacht for sale.

Generally speaking, in motor cruisers the most desirable features are twin-screws, diesels with single lever controls, ideally linked to an inside and outside steering position. On sailing auxiliaries, the requirements are parallel. Again, it is diesels which most people want, but here the most favoured type is a light, compact engine with a really good power/weight ratio. A single lever control is also looked upon with great favour, and unobtrusiveness is much in demand.

Petrol engines come second in popularity. This type is generally entirely acceptable in small cruisers where the fuel consumption in a year will not amount to more than, say, 60 gallons. Auxiliary yachts, in particular cruiser/racers and very small auxiliaries (that is, under 4 tons) are very frequently found with petrol engines because the power/weight ratio is good. The requirement here is very much for compactness, whilst fuel costs are almost negligible.

Petrol/paraffin engines are currently right out of favour. However, recent technical developments are offered in some makes of paraffin engines which require no petrol to start them and this type may swing back into favour.

When dealing with diesel engines in the 40–180 horsepower range, there is a broad division which has a strong influence on price. On the one hand, there are the mass-produced inexpensive diesels based on automotive engines. These engines are made in enormous numbers for tractors, cars and lorries, and a small proportion of the total output are adapted for marine purposes. These engines are quite cheap and so highly developed that they are normally most reliable. They give a good power/weight ratio and anyone looking for plenty of horsepower per £ expenditure should certainly go for this type. Typical prices are £500 for 50 horsepower; in contrast there are available the heavier, more expensive engines which have the reputation of being good, long-lasting 'sloggers'. Their price can be three, and even five times, greater than the automotive engines. Their power/weight ratio is not so good but they can claim great reliability. In the past this type had the same sort of following that a Rolls-Royce car has. People with plenty of money have gone for them, partly for their reliability, partly for the prestige, partly for the fact that they last so long and, partly, for the fine engineering.

But 'the old order changeth'. People are now realising that for one of these very fine engines it is possible to buy three, or even five, of the cheaper ones. The cheaper ones have reached a pinnacle of reliability not far short of that achieved by the 'sloggers'. Some people owning twin-screw yachts save money by putting in two of the cheap automotive type engines and buying a complete spare engine, maybe even two spares, instead of fitting a pair of the more expensive type.

The great curse of all diesels at the moment is their high noise level. Here the slogging, relatively slow running engines are usually better than the automotive type. However, even here 'the old order changeth'. Designers and owners are realising that for economy and quietness the clever thing to do is to fit an automotive type diesel with a throttle setting which keeps it well below its top revs. This gives a relatively light, compact engine which puts out ample horsepower. By avoiding the big revs, that shrill scream combined with the well-known diesel 'knock', is much modified and so, here again, the lighter, fast-running, engine is ousting the heavier type.

One of the main reasons why the lighter type of engine is becoming so popular, apart from its price and compactness, is that yachts tend to run, at most, 20 hours each weekend for 25 weekends each year. The slogging type of engine is designed to run for literally hundreds of thousands of hours with very little maintenance. But this is not what the yachtsman wants. His engine will corrode away long before it wears out in many instances.

All these considerations must be borne in mind when looking at a second-hand yacht, or ordering a new one.

Another factor comes into the matter. The automotive type of diesel is relatively cheap to maintain while the slogging type is expensive in spares, is often bulky and heavy, and cannot be lifted out of a boat unless good tackle is available. The lighter type of engine is that much easier to lift out and, as with a motor car, it often makes sense to get a replacement engine instead of doing even a moderate overhaul after, say, four or maybe seven years running.

Naturally, the ease with which the engine can be lifted in and out affects the overhauling costs. This is worth remembering when building a new, or looking at a second-hand, boat.

There is another quite separate aspect which must be considered in this matter of favoured engines. In the last 20 years there has been a rapid increase in the amount of horsepower owners demand in all types of yachts. Twenty-five years ago a 40-ft motor cruiser might have been built with two 25 horsepower engines, whereas now she will have two 50, or maybe two 100s, even though she is a 'displacement' and not a planing type of yacht.

In the same way, a 7-ton auxiliary sailing yacht would often have been fitted with 4 or 8 horsepower. Now plenty come out with 24 horsepower. By using automotive type engines which rev fairly fast to give a good power/weight ratio, it is possible to fit an old boat with two or three times its former horsepower, still in the same space.

One result of this is that the price of an old boat can be much influenced by the horsepower fitted. These days the demand is for the maximum speed that can be squeezed out of the hull under power, regardless of the fact that doubling the horsepower often gives only one extra knot. In some ways, this big increase in horsepower does make sense because the older boats tended to be under-powered when faced with a strong head wind and heavy seas. In particular, sailing yachts of all sizes built 20 years ago seldom had enough engine power to drive them against a gale, except perhaps in very sheltered waters. Nowadays, it is not unusual to see sailing yachts thrashing dead to windward against a screaming gale with no sails up, while the engine does its damndest. Certainly, this is one way of being sure of getting back on time for work on Monday morning.

In this matter of horsepower, it is worth noting that a 8-horsepower diesel engine for an auxiliary of between 5 and 10 tons, or a motor cruiser between 20 and 30 ft overall, can cost as much as a 24-horsepower petrol engine. Admittedly the latter uses more fuel but it can always be run slowly. And in the course of a season fuel costs anyhow make relatively little difference in this power range.

Yet another type of engine is the small air-cooled petrol unit of between 1–6 horsepower. The characteristics here are light weight, a good power/weight ratio, normally achieved by fast running, and a very low initial cost. This type does not shine in the reliability stakes. It is the sort of engine fitted in little launches which are used in sheltered waters, also in auxiliary cruisers up to about 4 tons and, maybe, on a cruiser/racer where the owner is fanatically determined to save every ounce of weight but needs some form of machinery to get him home in a flat calm. Very often the clever thing to do here is to throw away the whole power unit and fit a new one every three years. Spending little money on maintenance but using this throw-away technique, it is possible to keep engine costs down to £15 per year, since the new basic power unit is available for as little as £45. It must be realised that when buying and installing an engine, the power plant is only half the total cost in this size range, the rest of the expense coming from the propeller, shaft, tube, petrol tank, silencer, exhaust, controls, engine bearers, installation labour, and so on. The replacement of the power plant is so simple and quick that a throw-away technique, instead of elaborate maintenance, makes a lot of sense.

First cousins to the light air-cooled petrol engines are the air-cooled diesels and their half-sisters, the water-cooled diesel engines up to about 10 or 15 horsepower.

These engines are often marinised versions of industrial power units. Manufacturers produce basic engines which are used for a variety of purposes such as builders' plant and farm machinery. A small percentage are completed for use in yachts. I have run one in my own boat for five years and it is fairly typical. It is known affectionately as 'the concrete mixer', since its sister engines are to be seen on any building site. It's noisy, rather heavy for the horsepower it puts out, and relatively bulky. I am happy to accept its disadvantages because it is quite fantastically reliable and astonishingly cheap to run. To give an example of this, it is used every weekend throughout a summer season (say 24 weekends), also for a fortnight's holiday every year. Naturally one uses the engine as little as possible in a sailing yacht, but it has to run sometimes right through 8-hour calms. In a season it costs approximately £7 for fuel and annual maintenance; the latter being almost negligible.

This type of engine cannot be squeezed into a light displacement sailing yacht and it lacks the punch for any motor cruiser, except something quite small – say under 24 ft. It has also another minor disadvantage, in that it requires strong, carefully fitted engine bearers, because it is heavy and 'packs a punch'.

It is significant that this type of engine is fitted in charter boats which put in four times as much work each year as the average yacht. However, plenty of time and money needs to be spent on soundproofing.

When assessing an engine installation, a lot of experience is needed to tell whether the work has been well done. And without taking the head off the engine and getting involved in a lot of laborious stripping down, it is hard to assess the engine's worth. However, much can be guessed if the fuel pipes are kinked, if the electric wiring hangs in festoons, and if the controls consist of those dreadful plain steel, fast-rusting, inner and outer cable type fittings, which are only suitable for vehicles.

An installation where the controls are smooth and properly linked by rods rather than wire starts off on the right foot. If the engine has holding-down bolts with locking nuts, if the exhaust pipe has a flexible section and a well fastened silencer, if the fuel tank is really rigid, then the engineer probably knew his job. If there is no wear at the propeller shaft or the stern bearings, if the propeller blade and edges are free from chips and kinks, then this happy state of affairs is probably reflected in the rest of the machinery. But beware the cunning owner who has read this book before you. He will have stripped off the valve cover, the gear lever, the water pump and other portable parts, given the engine a wipe over, taken home the parts he has removed and given them a high-gloss enamel finish. He will also take home the copper pipes and burnish them till they shine like copper kettles. When all these pieces are put back you will get the impression that the engine is treated with constant loving care. Whereas, of course, the truth may be that he is trying to mislead you into buying.

16 *Paying for the boat and chartering her out*

'Raising the wind' is the universal problem. A very large number of people looking for a boat have, in the Bank, say £700. Within a few days of starting the search, they find that all possible boats which come within their requirements cost £1,000. This situation varies at all levels. One may scale it down to £70 in the Bank, or up to £7,000, or £70,000. It may be some consolation to a buyer to know that the very wealthy appear to have all their money sunk in some factory, oil-well, or similar enterprise. Sometimes even people internationally known for their wealth make use of financing facilities when it comes to buying a boat.

We will assume that the boat has been found and she is in every way suitable. All that remains is to find enough money to pay for her. One approach is to offer the owner a proportion of the money at once and the rest to be paid in subsequent months or years. This is a rare method of financing, but if the owner is having trouble selling he may jump at the opportunity. From the buyer's point of view, it is very attractive since he is virtually borrowing money from the seller at no interest rates. It is essential to have a legal document covering the situation which is mutually satisfying to both sides. Above all, the ownership must be clearly established, the boat must be very fully insured and the insurance company should be told of the situation, just to be on the safe side. Another method is to form a partnership, and this is the subject of a separate chapter.

A fairly common approach is to get an overdraft from a Bank. An extraordinary situation arises here in that at present, the Banks do not seem willing to take yachts as security. Bankers apparently do not appreciate that yachts can be very fully insured, are seldom total losses, are very seldom stolen and when they are, are usually recovered. It seems that anybody wanting to borrow money from the bank must put up other security, since banks are disinclined to take the yacht herself as collateral. With the current re-thinking going on in banking circles, it is possible that within the next few months, or years, bankers may become more enlightened.

The great attraction of a bank overdraft is that interest is only paid on the actual overdraft. Every pound paid into the bank reduces the debt and, hence, interest.

A mortgage is in strong contrast to a bank loan because interest rates are paid on the whole mortgage, i.e. the initial sum borrowed throughout the life of the mortgage. Thus, a three-year mortgage at 5% on a £1,000 involves paying £50 interest each year for three years, even though at the end of one year £333 6s 8d is paid off. The same sum is paid off at the end of the second year, but the total interest per annum does not reduce. Another disadvantage of a mortgage is that the yacht must be registered. In Great Britain, only a British subject can own a British registered yacht. If there are two or more owners, they all must be British.

In this instance, the word 'British' covers Dominion and Colonial citizens. There is a simple way round this problem for non-British subjects. They form a British company and the company owns the yacht. The directors' nationality is immaterial.

If the yacht is an old one she may be difficult, if not impossible, to register since everyone who has ever owned her must be traced and each transfer Bill of Sale produced for the Registration Authorities. The work can take a lot of time and can cost a great deal of money. In short, mortgages tend to be sometimes tedious, rather slow to bring to fruition and often quite expensive in legal fees.

McGruers of Clynder, Dumbartonshire built this 47′ 3″ yawl. She is 33′ long on the waterline, and represents the acme of superb yacht construction. A yacht of this calibre will cost between £15,000 and £27,000, the final price depending on the number, type and quality of the fittings and detail finish.

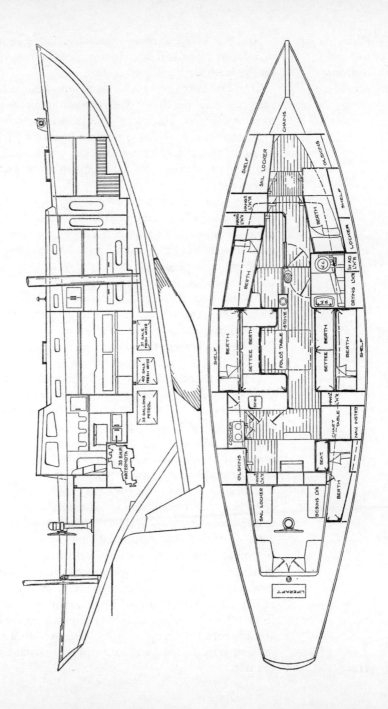

35 GALS.
PETROL

40 GALS.
FRESH WATER

37 GALS.
FRESH WATER

35 B.H.P.
WATERMOTA

CHAINS

SHELF

SAIL LOCKER

OILSKINS

HANG'
LKR

BERTH

SHELF

BERTH

OIL LOCKER

INF'AD
LKR

DRYING LKR

SHELF

BERTH

SETTEE BERTH

FOLD'G TABLE

STOVE

SETTEE BERTH

BERTH

SHELF

COOKER

SINK

HANG'G
LKR

CHART
TABLE LKR

NAV. INSTR'S

OILSKINS

HANG'
LKR

SEAT

SAIL LOCKER

BC'SUN'S LKR

BERTH

LIFERAFT

Hire Purchase is another alternative. The snag here is that the interest rate is often high, indeed in some cases it can be particularly stiff, up to 12%.

To make matters worse, in some instances the 12% is paid on the full purchase price and throughout the whole term of the loan. This means that for an owner buying a £2,000 boat and putting down a deposit of £1,000, he pays interest amounting to £120 per annum from the date of purchase to the completion of the H.P. agreement.

There are, of course, other sources of money, a popular one being a loan from an Insurance Company, using an existing life assurance policy as security. The snag here is that the policy must usually have been running for a period of two or three years, varying according to the Assurance Company.

All this boils down to the fact that the yacht buyer should shop around the various sources of cash, since each has its advantages and disadvantages.

As the law stands at present, there is a measure of tax relief on mortgage interest payments.

In other chapters it has been categorically stated that a buyer should only use 85% of his available funds for the purchase of a yacht. In certain circumstances, the phrase 'available funds' should be taken as including not only cash in hand but also money that can be borrowed. For example, a man with a wife and two children may have £700 in the bank. If he tries to buy a cruiser for this sum, he may too easily end up with a cramped, poor performing miniature cruiser, or a decrepit old boat. Both are not good 'buys', in three cases out of five. If this man could borrow another £700 he would probably get a vastly better boat. She would give him more fun, probably depreciate less, be safer, instil much greater pride of ownership, and so on. The argument in favour of the bigger boat at these price levels is pretty overwhelming. In this instance the buyer would probably put up say £470, leaving a little money in hand for essential alterations and repairs and borrow the rest.

Thrusting into every part of yachting is the trend towards multihulls. These are sometimes twin-hulled, called catamarans, or triple-hulled, like this trimaran. She is built by Honnor Marine, of Totnes, Devon. This type gives a high average speed, and heels over very little, even when driven hard.

The Rapier 3100 is built to designs by Cox and Haswell, of Parkstone Road, Poole, Dorset. Intended for coastal fast cruising, she will do over thirty knots, so could be used for water-skiing. Her price ranges from £8,500 to £9,500 according to the specification.

Ayrshire Maid and a typical modern small fibreglass cruiser. These two yachts represent 70 years of progress in yacht-building.

For the owner who wants everything, the 46 ft. Rapier 4600 is hard to beat. She will do more than 22 knots, has a full complement of electronic gear, and is built to Lloyds. There are two double cabins, a separate foc's'le for the paid hand, and a spacious deck saloon. Her price would be about £34,000 depending on the final finish. Designers are Cox and Haswell, of Parkstone Road, Poole.

When buying a yacht, it is worth asking if she has a cradle, since it may add to her value and make her easier to lay up. Ask too about the cost of launching off, since a simple lift by a crane is usually much cheaper than the old-fashioned business of moving a boat on skids across the yard and down the beach.

A converted racing boat, like this ex-6 metre, makes a fast though rather wet cruiser. The short cabin-top highlights another disadvantage, the space below decks is limited, but then prices for this type are often very low too.

In general, whatever the source of finance, it is usually necessary to pay off within three years. Every astute financier (at all levels from schoolboy to millionaire) will know that the clever thing to do if running out of finance is to re-finance from another source after, say, 2 years to pay off the original loan and thus have an extra 18 months to pay.

There are plenty of people who feel that a boat should not be bought unless the full purchase price is readily available. With this attitude I fully sympathise. It is noteworthy that in Britain the further north one goes from the Thames, the more reluctant people are to get involved in loans of any sort for boats. Finance companies with offices north of Hadrian's Wall will tell you that yacht mortgage is much rarer in Scotland than in England. It may well be, therefore, that an owner needs an argument to convince his own conscience, or maybe his mother-in-law, that he is justified in borrowing money to buy a boat. Undoubtedly, the best argument is that yacht owners do not spend money on expensive hotel or continental holidays; they go sailing instead and at holiday time save what others dissipate.

Furthermore it is common sense that a yacht is ideal for teaching children self-reliance and similar virtues. Any boat gets its owner and his family off the death-ridden roads, gives pleasant exercise, adventure, and endless enjoyment.

Another method of paying for a yacht is to charter her out. The snag here is that she is not available to her owner when she is away on charter, and most charter parties will only pay the day before they go aboard. However, the owner who is prepared to miss four weeks of his sailing season, provided he can find four reliable charterers, can make around a minimum of £8 per berth per week, without effort, at any good yachting centre. This figure is a very approximate one and, in general, privately chartered yachts might be expected to fetch 20% less per berth per week than the charter companies charge. It must be squarely faced that many charter parties leave boats dirty, and at least slightly chipped or damaged. Sometimes they leave her far from her home moorings, away down wind.

Another very important point to watch when chartering yachts out is that the insurance fully covers the situation. Normally the Insurance Company will require an additional premium.

Quite a few owners manage to pay all their annual fitting out expenses from income made by chartering. They tend to get their boats afloat early, and keep them afloat fairly late. In this way they have the use of the boat for two weekends out of three when she is afloat. Another way of having the cake and eating it is to charter from Sunday evening to the following Friday evening. Naturally, one gets a lower rate for such an arrangement but it does mean that the owner is aboard, in any case, when the charter party arrive to take over. Likewise, when the owner comes down for his next weekend's sailing, his boat is just back on moorings.

This private chartering arrangement seems to work best when the same person, or party, charters the boat year after year. Each party knows the other's quirks. The charter party are used to the yacht and familiar with her gear.

Probably the very best people to charter a yacht from an owner are his regular crew. Even if the boat is on charter to a good friend, there should be a legal document, drawn up by a lawyer, not the owner, setting out all the conditions. Once this form has been professionally produced, it can be used again and again, just for the trouble of re-typing it and changing the appropriate date and name.

This document should cover all eventualities, such as damage to the boat, non-return to moorings at the end of the charter period, loss of the dinghy or outboard, loss of life and limb on board, arbitration and so on. It is usual for the owner to request a deposit before the charter commences to pay for damage incurred and loss of gear.

It is also quite usual for the charter party to agree to a limited cruising ground. This both reduces the risks and also makes it reasonably sure the boat is back on her home moorings in due time.

17 *Partnerships and syndicates*

Sharing a yacht with another owner, even a close relative or friend, can be extremely difficult. Yachts generate many varied and deep emotions, from love to seasickness. This makes sharing hard, so that unsuccessful partnerships are more numerous than good ones.

However, in certain cases – and with sufficient precautions – partnerships are worth considering.

Where there is insufficient money to buy a boat, or where a yacht is to be owned by a man who cannot use it more than a few weekends every year, then partnership may be the answer.

My experience, both in partnership and watching my friends and acquaintances as they struggle in dual harness, makes me convinced that the following rules must be followed:

1. The partnership must be as uneven as possible.
2. The finances must be most carefully managed.
3. Partners must share an intense interest in racing, in cruising, or in fishing. But if partners' interests are not the same, then trouble is inevitable.

Taking each of these essential basic precepts in turn; the ideal partnership seems to be between a man of vast experience who pays up to, say, 80% of the money, and a relative beginner who puts up the rest of the money. The major partner will be the skipper and dominate the situation. He will normally take the helm when entering and leaving harbour and at critical times. To a large extent the boat is his but he has the double advantage of not having to bear the full cost and maintenance expenses, and he is sure of a regular crew in the form of the second partner.

The junior partner has the use and pleasure of the yacht, yet he only has to find a fraction of the cost. If he has any sense, he will pick up a mass of knowledge

and experience and have a great deal of fun without
undue risk. He has the pride of ownership without the
full load of responsibility, and he will never spend a
weekend swinging round a mooring, worried because
it is blowing rather hard and he is not sure whether it is
safe to get under way. This uneven type of partnership
works at all levels, in racing dinghies, in cruisers and in
offshore racers. It can be extended to more than two
partners, provided that the basic concept of one completely dominating partner is maintained. However,
partnerships of three are bad, since there will be a
tendency for two to seem to be against one on too many
occasions.

The second rule concerns not only the account of the
monies involved, but also the preliminary planning on
expenditure. If there is one dominating partner who is
experienced, he can (and should) say at the beginning of
the season: 'I am putting up £150 for the boat's
maintenance this year; as you own a quarter, please put
in £50. This will cover all maintenance costs, including ... ' And here follows a precise list of the items
covered. The senior partner, being experienced, should
have a fairly accurate, though perhaps not precise, idea
of probable expenditure so that he can make up a good
preliminary list. He will know enough to allow 15%
extra for contingencies and, being experienced, he will
make certain the yacht is fully insured, the insurance
company being informed of the dual ownership.

During the course of the year, every item of expenditure is carefully accounted for. To avoid a lot of petty
accounting entries, the yacht should be fully equipped
when launched in the Spring, with spare shackles, spare
rope, spare batteries and so on. But then, of course, all
properly fitted out yachts are so equipped!

If this is a racing partnership, then the facts of racing
must be looked squarely in the face. In the case of, say, a
Class III ocean racer, it must be agreed beforehand that,
for example, sail repairs and replacements will cost £150
per race.

If the maximum amount of financial pre-planning is

carried out and if the expenditure is carefully detailed, then the partnership will not founder for financial reasons. Otherwise, this is the most likely cause of trouble.

Another serious cause of friction is a mixture of interests. A cruising man will not want to spend money on spinnaker gear, whereas the racing man will not only want to buy spinnaker equipment but go for the lightest possible fittings. These will give you extra efficiency but, being lighter, they will break and so there will not only be the initial expenditure but also the replacement costs. A typical cruiser costs less than half as much to run per season as the equivalent size racing yacht, as a rough guide. So if one owner is interested in racing and the other hates it, the partnership will be over-stressed.

18 *Watching the building of a new boat*

Anyone buying a new boat is expending a lot of hard-earned money. It is natural to want to be quite sure that the boat is up to standard, well built, safe and likely to last a long time. I will not say 'free from all troubles' because a boat lives a hectic life, constantly at the mercy of the wind, sea, and its owner. All boats live a varied life, each with her fair share of the world's troubles.

During building, the work can be supervised by the owner, the designer, Lloyd's, or one of the other supervisory bodies, such as Bureau Veritas, or a yacht surveyor.

In practice, most owners like to keep an eye on the boat themselves, so far as is possible. This is one argument for building fairly near home, though in these days when air transport is so convenient and not all that expensive, the argument against building in a yard far from home is much reduced.

In my opinion every owner should, within reason, supervise the construction of his own boat. Not only will he learn a great deal about how she is put together, but also he will get an enormous amount of fun and interest through watching her grow.

Just as important, he will supervise those little finishing touches which everyone else will miss. He will be concerned with the *minute details* and his whole mind will be on the one boat. The same cannot be said of the professional people involved. Designers and surveyors usually have to watch *ten or twelve* boats at once.

The owner can over-surprise, by visiting the yacht every day and spending hours talking to everybody concerned, from the apprentices to the managing director. This is not fair on the yard as it wastes the men's time and distracts them from the job. A reasonable compromise would be a weekly visit. In the early stages of construction, once every two or three weeks will probably be enough, assuming the yacht takes six months to build.

If a designer is asked to supervise the construction of a boat his design fee will be increased by an amount which varies according to the size of the boat and her distance from the design office. In general, the design fee will be increased by about 50%, if supervision is included.

The designer will normally visit the yacht for a whole day about once every three or four weeks, again assuming she takes about six months to build. He will normally attend the launching and trials.

It is usually well worth while having the designer supervise the work. It may be superfluous if the yard has already built four or five identical boats, or if the yard is one of those big ones with very full supervisory staff where the owner will, anyhow, be paying a relatively high price for his boat.

Designers vary a good deal in the amount of supervision they give. For instance, I know of only three who will take the trouble to go up a sailing yacht's mast once the boat is afloat, to check that everything is safe and secure. This is one excellent reason why the owner should take more than a passing interest in the construction.

Very busy designers, and this usually means the most successful ones, naturally have less time available to look after the interests of one particular boat.

It makes a great deal of sense for the designer and the owner to visit the boat on the same day and, here again, it is far better to avoid Saturdays and Sundays whenever possible.

The construction of certain yachts is supervised by one of the specialist institutions. In Britain, Lloyd's pretty well dominate this field, and they also do a tremendous lot of work all over the world. On the continent, and very occasionally in Britain and elsewhere, larger yachts are supervised by Bureau Veritas and equivalent bodies abroad. But what is said in the following paragraphs about Lloyd's for big yachts applies to these other institutions.

In practice, Lloyd's appear to provide a more comprehensive service than any equivalent incorporated body in other countries. Any yacht built to the International Racing Rules, such as the 5·5 metre class, the 7 and 8 metre cruiser/racers' 12 metres to the International Rule and so on, *must* be built to Lloyd's scantling Rules and under the supervision of a Lloyd's surveyor in order to obtain a Racing Certificate.

The majority of yachts over 50 tons are built to Lloyd's scantlings. However, these scantlings are merely published lists of suitable thicknesses and sizes of planking, plating, frames' fastenings and so on. A yacht may be built to these scantlings without at the same time being supervised by a Lloyd's surveyor.

When a boat is for sale, one sometimes sees the phrase 'Built to Lloyd's'. This means that she has been built both to Lloyd's scantlings and under their supervision. Sometimes the phrase used is 'Built in excess of Lloyd's'. This implies that the scantlings are bigger than Lloyd's specify, but does not actually state that Lloyd's supervised the work. In my opinion it is a slightly two-faced remark since heavy scantlings, not carefully fashioned and fabricated, are found in some rough, shoddy boats which lack strength and seaworthiness, even though their planking and frames are quite massive. However, for deep sea cruising it is a very comforting thought if the scantlings are extra heavy.

If a boat is to be built under Lloyd's supervision, then the designer has to write either to Lloyd's Register of Shipping, 71 Fenchurch Street, London, EC3, asking for Form Surveys 6, or apply to a local provincial office. Lloyd's will require the designer to supply in triplicate the main construction drawings and such plans as the rudder and steering arrangements, also the fuel tank plans and so on. They lay down no rules for the rig and rigging, so their interest virtually ceases above the chain plates.

Having examined the plans and made sure the scantlings are equal to or equivalent to Lloyd's scantling table for that size of yacht, the surveyor will then give approval for construction to begin. It is quite likely that the designer will want to introduce his latest ideas into the boat's construction. If Lloyd's do not approve this, then they will mark the plans in red and the designer must make modifications. All this takes time and costs money. The fees charged by Lloyd's for the survey and classification of yachts fills a whole booklet. This booklet only covers surveys which take place in England, east of a line from the Wash to Weymouth and in the main yacht-building area of mid-Clyde region. Surveys outside this area will cost more because travelling expenses are added on. The following are typical of the charges:

For Steel yachts

5 tons	£50
15 tons	£100
50 tons	£187 10
100 tons	£300

Wood and Composite yachts are as above, but increased by 20%.

For yachts of the International Racing Classes:

5·5 metres	£35
8 metres	£45
12 metres	£70

For Reinforced Plastic yachts: for supervision of Hull Moulding

Up to 20 ft	£22 (minimum fee)
Up to 40 ft	£38
Up to 60 ft	£60

For Completion to Class of a Hull which has been Moulded under Supervision:

Up to 20 ft	£20
40 ft	£31
60 ft	£56

For Catamarans and Trimarans:

	CATAMARANS		TRIMARANS	
RULE LENGTH	*Steel and Reinforced Plastic*	*Wood*	*Steel and Reinforced Plastic*	*Wood*
Ft	£ s d	£ s d	£ s d	£ s d
20	48 0 0	54 0 0	58 0 0	66 0 0
30	64 5 0	72 10 0	78 0 0	89 0 0
40	80 10 0	91 0 0	98 0 0	112 0 0
50	96 15 0	109 10 0	118 0 0	135 0 0
60	148 0 0	167 10 0	180 10 0	206 10 0

NOTE: The above scale covers both the survey during construction and the completion to class of the hulls.

Yachts built to Lloyd's Rules, if they are to keep their Class – which might be described as their pedigree – have to be surveyed at regular intervals.

An indication of the charges is given hereunder for a Wood or Composite Yacht:

Between 5–10 tons   £8 for the Biennial Survey
Between 20–25 tons   £17 for the Biennial Survey
Between 50–75 tons   £24 for the Biennial Survey

Steel yachts are slightly less.

Lloyds do not guarantee that a boat will be fast, or easy to handle, or good to look at, or even reach a specified speed under power. They will not even guarantee that her mast will stay up in a Force 5 breeze. But they do give her a pedigree which covers the quality of most of the material used in the construction. They also keep an eye on the standard of work put into the hull, deck and deckhouses.

The yacht's designer, when supervising construction is likely to take a more detailed interest in the boat. The same applies to a *yacht* surveyor, when supervising construction. A *ships'* surveyor does not have the technical knowledge, and seldom the seagoing experience in small boats necessary for this job.

A good designer or surveyor will check such things as the locking of the rigging screws, the lead of the anchor chain to the winch, the risk of riding turns on the sheet winch and the accessibility of the lavatory seacocks. A good supervising surveyor may even go aloft once the mast is in place for a check on all the fittings. If he does not, then the owner should (or he should send his son aloft since that is what yachtsmen have sons for).

In conclusion, it can be stated that no supervision is continuous. Very few designers can visit a boat more than once a fortnight. A weekly visit is occasionally possible, but even that means only one day in five. It therefore boils down to the fact that supervision is highly desirable but, of itself, not enough. The way to get a good new boat is to have her built at an established yard with a high reputation. Here, the management has years of experience, plenty of sea-time and, often enough, everybody concerned has been in the business five generations and a couple of hundred years. What is more, they have every intention of staying at the top of the boatbuilding business.

The survey

SURVEY FEES

Minimum Fee £15

5 tons	£20	11 tons	£37	16 tons	£47
6 "	£23	12 "	£39	17 "	£49
7 "	£26	13 "	£41	18 "	£51
8 "	£29	14 "	£43	19 "	£53
9 "	£32	15 "	£45	20 "	£55
10 "	£35				

Thereafter rate is £2 per ton up to 50 tons.
In excess of 50 tons, the rate is 30/– per ton.

If there is one piece of advice that really matters in this whole book, it is 'Have a *proper* survey before buying'. More trouble is caused through not having a survey than all other causes put together. After all, if you buy a boat that does not suit your needs, then you sell her, and with little loss unless the market has collapsed meanwhile, which is a rare event. But if you buy a boat that you find later is riddled with defects, then almost all your money is straight down the drain.

A survey is a very cheap form of insurance. However, it is more than that. If you decide to sell your boat after a few years, and can show a prospective buyer both the survey report you had when you bought her, as well as your yard bills, he can see that the boat should be in top condition. He can see the defects your surveyor listed, when you bought the boat, and set against these the various repair items in your yard bills. In a few minutes he can see that you have been looking after the boat conscientiously. For this reason, it is sensible to keep the survey report after you have bought the boat.

Another reason why you should have a full survey is

that as a document it makes bargaining infinitely easier. You may feel that the boat is worth £1,800. The owner is asking, perhaps, £2,200, and after a little negotiating he may come down to £2,000. You will have based your judgement of the boat's worth on what you have seen of her. The owner may not have seen her for over a year (he may have been abroad), or he may, like most owners, see her through rose-coloured spectacles. His pride in his boat biases him so much that he sees no more than half her defects. He genuinely may not know about those four cracked frames down in the tuck. Plenty of owners never do rootle down under the engine and if they do they fail to see the cracked frames. You can mention to the owner that you have seen the cracked frames, but he will just think you are trying to knock the price and may not budge. Or he may not budge much. But once he has seen a survey report, he is likely to take a different view.

Here it must be mentioned that a full thorough survey on any yacht more than eight or ten years old can be a highly disconcerting bit of literature. It is enough to make anyone weep. It goes on and on, telling of splits in coamings, open seams, loose rudder bearings, signs of movement at beam ends, rusted stanchion feet, loose fuel tanks, and there is seldom a word of praise for the boat. But that is the whole point. Anything not mentioned is assumed either to be inaccessible to the surveyor, or found to be in good condition.

The report that a surveyor sends out varies a great deal according to who does the job. Surveying is a blend of science and art, and so these reports are as varied as any other works of art. For a start, one famous surveyor considers that he has made a full report if he covers one side of a foolscap sheet of paper, the typing being double spaced, for a yacht of five tons. My own report on a yacht of this size normally runs to five foolscap sheets, close typed. Then again, some surveyors make no mention at all of the yacht's engine. This is because it is usual to have an entirely separate survey of the engine where this is required. My own experience is that except in the cases of motor yachts over 40 tons owners do not want to pay the extra for an engine survey. At the same time, they would like to know a bit about the engine and its installation. Therefore, without dismantling the engine, I try and list as much information about the machinery as I can. It is usually possible to tell if the engine has been well installed and properly looked after by such indicators as the standard of piping and wiring, the cleanliness of the engine, its drip tray, the presence of corrosion on the batteries, and so on.

At the beginning of this chapter is a scale of the standard survey fees. There are retired inshore fishermen, enthusiastic amateur surveyors and others who will do the job for less. If you really feel that you can trust their judgement and experience, or lack of it, then go ahead and take the risk. One snag is that some of them will not put their signatures at the foot of their report. Another, more serious, is that even if they do sign the report, it carries little or no weight.

Among the advantages of going to a qualified surveyor there is the consultation after you have had time to read and digest the report. Most surveyors will spend half an hour with you, going through the report either in their office or over the telephone. There may be words you do not understand, which is not something to be ashamed of, because boat-building terms vary from county to county. For instance, that length of timber which runs from bow to stern, inside the top plank is known in different areas as: Beam shelf, Beam stringer, Beam ledge, Upper Stringer, and sometimes just as the shelf.

This talk with the surveyor is sometimes very valuable, because he may be able to tell you more than he can, or is prepared to, write down. The boat he is surveying may be one of a class in which he races. He may have owned her once, or her sister-ship. He may have helped build her, or been apprenticed to the man who designed her. Yacht designing and building is a fairly small world. An experienced surveyor has in his head a big store of knowledge, folk-lore based on tales which have a good foundation of fact, as well as experience afloat, knowledge of owners and how they maintain and sail their craft, and so on. So get him to talk if he will.

But don't expect too much from him. No surveyor should be expected to answer the question 'Shall I buy this boat' simply because the question is too personal. He can put all the facts before you, put the proper emphasis on them, but the final judgement must be yours.

There is another question which cannot fairly be asked of the surveyor, namely: 'What is the value of this yacht that you have surveyed?' A valuation is a long and sometimes difficult task. In these days of galloping inflation, erratic markets and many cross-currents, a valuation takes a lot of work and cross-checking. To ask for all this work to be done for nothing, and at a moment's notice, is tantamount to asking a shopkeeper to give away his stock.

The way to approach the problem is this. After the surveyor has done his job, and when you have talked the report over with him, tell him the price you are going to pay. Ask him if that is about right. He can reasonably be expected to say the price is about right, sounds high, or is maybe something of a bargain. But he can also quite fairly say that he has no idea. If you want a valuation, it is worth first asking how much this will cost. It can be a valuable financial advantage to have a certified valuation, for Death Duty, Capital Gains Tax and other situations. For instance, if you insure the boat for her certified valuation figure no Insurance Company can claim you have over or under-insured.

If a boat is only one or two seasons old, a buyer may feel that she is bound to be in good condition, and that a survey is just a waste of money. Quite the contrary is the case. The seller may tell you that he is getting rid of the boat solely because she is too small. The truth may be that she has had rot built into her, and he is getting shot of her rather than bear the expense of putting the defects right. It is rare these days for rot to be built into a boat, though it does happen. It is not all that rare for a boat only a couple of years old to have rot in her. Wood rot, being a disease, attacks new as well as old boats, just as other diseases attack young and old people.

Before doing a survey on a yacht, the owner's permission should be obtained. The buyer, or his broker, gets this and it should be in writing. This is because a survey inevitably slightly marks a boat. One of the skills of surveying is to find out a lot of information yet leave the boat only very slightly marked, so that after the Spring repaint, there is no indication that she has been surveyed.

In order that a survey can be thorough, some preparatory work must be done on many boats. Panelling has to be removed, if it is very extensive, so that the surveyor can get at the frames and the inside of the planking. Of course, a yacht like a Dragon has no panelling, but it may have well screwed-down floorboards. These will need taking up before the surveyor arrives, otherwise he will spend his time, and your money, doing work better and more cheaply done by a shipwright.

On many cruisers, tanks need to be taken out. Here a good surveyor can save a buyer a lot of money, by avoiding taking up tanks which are not strictly necessary. On the other hand, if you want the boat for long-range ocean cruising, where no tiny detail can be neglected, then all the tanks must come out.

If the yacht is carvel planked, her planks are likely to have screws at each end, into the stem and transom, sternpost, and so on. These fastenings are obviously very important, and are liable to de-zincing. If the boat is built regardless of cost, she may have had bronze screws put in her hood ends. However, even the best yards have used, and still do use, common brass screws. Due to the interaction of seawater and dissimilar metals, the brass loses its zinc and the screws become porous, brittle coppery ghosts, with little strength. So it is usual for a shipwright to take out a selection of these hood-end fastenings for the surveyor to examine. Occasionally it is policy to have the rudder removed prior to a survey, but usually only for a yacht to be used for ocean cruising.

On both power and sailing yachts which have ballast keels it is normal for a keel-bolt to be withdrawn for the surveyor's inspection. This is a job which can take most of a day, so all the preliminary work must be done well before the surveyor arrives. The examination of a keel bolt is something that is scarcely necessary if the bolts are bronze (as they normally are with a lead keel) and provided that the boat is no more than four years old. Or it may be that there is clear proof that the bolts have been examined, or renewed within the last season or two. In such a case it is sometimes the practice not to have a bolt out for examination.

Naturally the buyer pays for the work of removing and replacing panelling, hood-end fastenings and so on, even if the sale does not go through.

To make a full examination of a yacht's sails is sometimes extremely difficult in a yacht yard. The job can only be done properly if the sails are spread out completely, and very few yards have a dry, clean, covered space extensive enough. Most surveyors examine the sails as best they can, particularly at the corners where much of the wear occurs. They sometimes take note of the sail-maker and age of the sails, which have a bearing on the value of the sails, and hence on the overall condition of the yacht. It is quite usual for the surveyor to note that the sails 'need attention', or that they 'appear to have life in them' or some such phrase. The implication here is that the sails will do for cruising for a year or two at least, probably more. But it also means, even if the surveyor does not mention the fact, that a sail-maker should be asked to overhaul the sails and do the usual minor repairs before the yacht is put into commission.

A surveyor cannot state how many years sails can be expected to last because owners treat sails in very different ways. Some owners sail 4,000 miles in a season, in all weathers, and omit minor repairs so that small troubles compound. Others treat their sails like babies and make them last twenty years and more.

What with paying for the shipwright's work, as well as the surveyors, some buyers may wonder if it truly is worth having a survey. To show just how valuable a survey can be, there was the case of a 45-ft motor cruiser on the market. She was an old boat, but roomy. The seller asked £3,750 but there were no takers for some time. A buyer eventually came along and put up a bid of £3,000, subject to survey, pointing out that there was at least £400 worth of work to be done on the boat to make her seaworthy. The seller agreed to pay half the necessary £400 if the sale price was agreed at £3,200. A survey duly took place and showed that, apart from the £400 that certainly had to be spent on the boat, there was rot in the top planking, port and starboard, also in the covering board aft, port and starboard, with possibly more trouble inside but inaccessible.

Without comment the buyer sent a copy of the survey report to the seller. By return, the seller said that he would let the boat go for £2,300, provided he had no outlay on repairs. The buyer agreed and by employing his own shipwright, also by working on the yacht himself, he did *all* the repairs for around £500. He later reckoned his survey saved him quite £300. Other similar cases could be quoted.

20 *After you have bought her*

She's yours! You feel wildly excited, half your age, and nothing is going to stop you leaping aboard, throwing the moorings over and hurtling off for the distant horizon!

Will you kindly do no such thing. Please come quietly back to earth, repress your excitement and plough through a little paperwork.

The inventory should be checked against the equipment actually on board. There should be a full set of safety gear, including flares and day signals, life-jackets and life-buoys. *

At the same time, the insurance should be arranged. It is not possible to transfer an insurance policy from one owner to another. The reason is that the insurance company takes into account, not only the yacht, her condition, age and type, but also the owner's experience and previous record.

The insurance should be arranged through a company used to yachts and not big ships. There is a world of difference between the problems of the commercial shipping world and the average yachtsman. Typical of this is the importance of having extra Third Party insurance up to £50,000 for a boat of, say, 6 tons or less, and up to £100,000 for a bigger boat.

The reason for the extra is simple, but vital. It works like this: If a yacht is insured for her value of £1,000, then virtually under no conditions will the insurance company pay out more than £1,000 on any one claim. Should this yacht ram a bigger yacht and sink her, then the claim for the total loss of the bigger yacht may be £15,000. The owner of the small yacht, if proved to be at fault, would get £1,000 from the insurance company and would have to find the remaining £14,000 out of his own pocket. For about thirty shillings per

* See the R.Y.A. booklet *Water Wisdom*.

year many yacht insurance companies will offer the additional £25,000 cover, and this surely is the best value in the world.

This brings up a point about the cost of insurance. As in everything else, there are cheap policies which are frighteningly dangerous or, alternatively, more expensive policies which are very sound. It is worth remembering that in the event of an accident the owner and crew will be mentally distressed, possibly cold, wet, tired and in need of quite a lot of outside assistance. Under these conditions, the most one may be able to do is to telephone the broker or the local office of the insurance company and get instant, copious help, without question. This is what the good insurance companies do.

Other points to watch when insuring, include:

1. Personal gear requires extra insurance.
2. Outboard motors often require separate insurance and most companies require that they be chained on to the boat to prevent loss overboard.
3. Sails and spars are not normally covered for racing but special supplements to most policies are available.
4. The name of the yacht and her port must be on all of the ship's boats if the insurance is to cover these boats.
5. Ship's boats capable of high speeds, usually defined as 20 m.p.h. are not covered by the insurance unless special provision is made for them.

From all this, it will be seen why it is well worth insuring through a yacht broker or a naval architect who specialises in yachts. Insurance brokers (who may know all the snags about house policies or life insurance) can offer the wrong advice, or omit an important consideration, such as the extra Third Party cover.

Responsibility for the yacht is assumed by the buyer at the date of purchase. This means that the insurance should commence on that date, at an exact time of day agreed between buyer and seller so that there is not even an hour when the boat is uninsured. If this seems to be carrying things to excess, I recall one instance when a boat was left uninsured for only 24 hours and she must have known about it. She was almost new, with gleaming varnished topsides. She took it into her head to hit a navigation buoy and the damage was devastating. It cost about a third of her value to repair her.

Yard laying-up costs and mooring fees also commence at the date of purchase. If the boat is lying ashore, then the cost of launching her off is paid for by the buyer unless there is written agreement that the sale takes place with the boat afloat.

Some owners offer their boats for sale delivered afloat at any harbour within 200 or 500 miles of the laying-up yard. The reason is that their boats may be located away from the main yachting centres. They offer this additional attraction in order to get the boat sold. This sort of condition should be stated in writing as a condition of the sale.

If possible, having bought the boat, you should get the seller to come out for a trip. Get him to show you how to get the best out of the boat and any special tricks she may have. This is not a usual procedure, though Heaven knows why. Perhaps it is that so many boats are sold during the winter months when they are laid up ashore.

Go through the boat with the seller above and below decks. It is not unusual to find one little gadget aboard which defies all explanation. On long night watches, when alone at the helm, I still wonder about those two hooks on the Six-metre we once owned. They were located out on the covering board just ahead of the shrouds. Why, oh why, was the port one facing aft and the st'bd one facing forward? If only I had asked the previous owner what they were for! Provided, of course, *he* had remembered to ask *his* predecessor ...

21   *Names*

There is an old tradition that it is unlucky to change a yacht's name. In practice, relatively few owners buying a second-hand boat do change her name because boats are known, and usually admired, by a wide circle of yachtsmen. This means that by changing the name the yacht loses her identity. Her past racing successes are no longer associated with her so the new owner will not have the pleasure of hearing old hands reminiscing about how they once saw her thrashing down the Channel in the face of a Force 7, away out ahead of her rivals.

With a new boat, the problem of naming requires a good deal of thought. If the boat is called *Seamew*, then not surprisingly she will get muddled up with all the other boats of the same name.

Some owners find it extremely difficult to think of names and in this connection a family tradition is a great help. Possibly one of the most famous traditions is the Aisher family's succession of *Yeoman*'s. The difficulty here is that this family have built so many boats that they are at the present time up to about *Yeoman XV* so that mistakes and misunderstandings can occur.

The last three boats I have built for myself have been the *St Elizabeth*, *St Mary* and *St Hilary*, and even here I find our friends get muddled. However, there is little doubt as to who the original owner was!

When it comes to thinking up a name, there are a number of sources which are not overworked, such as the stars, flora, lepidoptera and similar wide ranging species. In Scotland, Ireland and Wales there is a tendency to use the old native tongues. But the problem here is pronunciation, not to mention the abstruse spelling.

A mixture of christian names is popular in America but tends to be either hackneyed or so obviously contrived.

'Lloyd's Register of Yachts' is a useful source of inspiration, even though it is discouraging because bright ideas are so often found to be already booked. The temptation to go for a pun or a joke should be strongly resisted. The joke wears thin within days, if not hours.

For an unregistered boat the problem of a suitable name is not truly serious, since the owner can use an existing name without worry, provided other boats of the same name are in remote sailing districts.

However, if a boat is to be registered, then her name must be acceptable to the Registrar of British Ships. This Authority will not accept an existing name, or even one very like it. To ask for the name *Seamew* is to invite rejection. However, the Registrar may accept *Seamew of Fambridge*, or *Blue Seamew* and this is the common way of getting around a recurring problem. In order to save time, most people send the Registrar a choice of three names in order of preference.

A boat's name should be shown clearly in bold letters on both sides of her cabin top, whether or not it is also on the transom. Very many transoms have a slope which makes it impossible for anybody on a quay to read the name. Now that there are so many yachts afloat and air-sea rescue searches have become a frequent occurrence round every coast, it is important for the authorities to be able to see quickly if a yacht, which is reported missing, is in fact safely tied up in some snug harbour.

At the moment yachting is mercifully free of legislation and restriction. If owners do not put the names on their yachts very clearly, then it will soon become compulsory to do so and in a short time licensing of yachts will follow. This will bring in its train all the misery attending the ownership of a car, with all its restrictions, taxation and bureaucratic paraphernalia.

Whenever a boat changes hands, the buyer should put down his money in exchange for a Bill of Sale (Individual or Joint Owners). This is the official form of receipt and it is well worth using even for a dinghy.

It establishes the owner's title to the boat and I have used it when cruising abroad when officials have asked to see the ship's papers.

It is Form No. 10, also headed No. 79 (Sale), and can be bought from H.M. Stationery Office, through professional stationery offices, or through a bookseller, for a few pence.

The Bill of Sale should be filled in as fully as possible. However, for an unregistered yacht there is no official number so the box at the top left-hand corner is left blank. Do not confuse the consecutive number in Lloyd's Register of Yachts with the official number. The consecutive number varies from year to year, since the number of yachts in Lloyd's annual register varies, and this consecutive number appears level with the yacht's name and above the official number. The consecutive number, of course, is merely a list number.

The name of the ship should be the name she has when you buy her, and underneath should be her former names, preceded by 'ex', thus:

Black Joker (ex-*Joker*, ex-*Seabird*)

The number, date and port of registry only apply to registered yachts. Her home port is not her port of registry.

The next box to be filled in is headed 'Whether a Sailing, Steam or Motor Ship' and here the criterion is the main motive power. In general, an auxiliary yacht will be listed as sail. 50–50 is obviously a borderline case, but if she is well canvassed and capable of clawing off a lee shore without engine, she is clearly a sailing yacht. However, a twin-screw 50–50 with little more than steadying canvas would be listed as a Motor Ship.

The final box in the top line is headed 'Horse Power of Engines, if any' and it is usual to list here the peak continuous output of the engine, as listed in the maker's catalogue.

When filling in the dimensions, note that the third line is depth inside and *not* draft, since this is a figure which must be measurable when the boat is afloat without special instruments.

When filling in the main body of the Bill of Sale, all one has to do is to follow the notes at the bottom. These are self-explanatory, except on the fifth line down where the words ' ... whereof is hereby acknowledged, transfer ... ' occur. In the blank space one fills in the words "sixty-four, sixty-fourths". This assumes that the owner is selling out completely to the buyer. But suppose the owner is now going into partnership with one other person and they are to have equal shares, then in the blank space after the word 'transfer' insert 'thirty-two, sixty-fourths'. Ships are traditionally divided into sixty-four shares, since this number is so conveniently sub-divided. I used to think that this was universally appreciated, but recently had to supply to the American customs a special letter of explanation, pointing out that yachts are not divided into one hundred parts but into sixty-four. So for selling a yacht to America, where there may be questions of Import Duty and so on, it may be advisable to cover the Bill of Sale with an explanatory letter.

The Bill of Sale establishes the buyer's title ' ... free from encumbrances'. This means that debts incurred by the vessel prior to the sale must be paid by the seller. It is well worth pointing out this fact to the seller and reminding him of his duties, if there is any doubt.

The seller signs at the bottom right-hand corner and not, as occasionally occurs by accident, at the bottom left-hand corner after the words 'Executed by the above-named'. After these words, the seller's full name should be put in, using capital letters and, indeed, it is customary to use block capitals throughout a Bill of

Sale. However, an even better procedure is to type the Bill of Sale where a long-carriage typewriter is available.

Only one witness is usual and he signs in the bottom left-hand corner where indicated. It is customary for the witness to be someone not a close relative of the seller, but the witness need not be a Justice of the Peace, or similar officer. There is space in the bottom right-hand corner for a seal, but I am bound to say that the big majority of Bills of Sale which I have seen have not been sealed. However, if I was travelling to 'far away places', where, from my experience, petty officials need impressing, I would most certainly put a big sealing wax seal in the appropriate place and would be sorely tempted to have strips of ribbon and additional seals, after the manner of ancient treaties. Apart from bottles of whisky as bribes, there is nothing so useful as a good, official-looking document when ocean cruising!

It is usual for the seller's broker to complete the Bill of Sale, and this office chore is one of the ways he earns his fee.

When the yacht is registered, the information on the Bill of Sale must exactly correspond to the details on the Certificate of Registry.

23   *Registration*

Yachting throws up all sorts of controversies. In fact, in the design office where I work it is held to be an extraordinary coincidence if three yachtsmen agree exactly on any one subject, and if four should be found to agree, then this comes into the category of miracles.

Registration is the subject of great controversy. As some people have an axe to grind in the matter, the controversy continues from year to year. Before listing the advantages and disadvantages of registration, it is worth clearing away a few popular misconceptions. A yacht is not registered just because her name appears in Lloyd's Register of Yachts. This excellent book is nothing more than a printed list of privately owned vessels. To be included in this list, a motorboat must be over 25 ft and a sailing boat must have a total sail area in excess of 300 sq ft. However, just to confuse the issue, anyone who owns a yacht falling short of these limits but who buys a copy of the Register can have his vessel included in its pages.

That thick green volume, Lloyd's Register, consists almost entirely of vessels owned in Great Britain, to-gether with a good proportion of Commonwealth and other yachts. In practice, this means that there are quite a few Australian and Canadian boats, with a smaller number of New Zealand and Carribean yachts. There are also quite a few European yachts listed.

A sister publication is the Lloyd's Register of American Yachts.

For a yacht to be *registered*, she must have an official certificate, which is like a birth certificate. She must also have her official number and nett registered tonnage carved on her main beam. However, just because she has a certificate, and has carvings on the main beam and so on, this does not mean that she is a thoroughbred, nor does it mean that she was necessarily well designed or even particularly well built.

In practice, most yachts over 12 tons are registered and most under 6 tons are not. In theory every yacht over 15 tons must be registered. But in practice some are not because they have been converted from service craft, or from fishing boats, or are home-built, and their owners have not known about the regulations. One reason why the smaller boats are seldom registered is the relatively high cost of the procedure and formalities. A major reason why bigger yachts are registered is that the owners wish to fly their Club's Blue ensign (assuming the owner's Club has such an ensign). In order to fly this flag, the owner must have an Admiralty Warrant which, incidentally, must be applied for in the case of each separate vessel the owner possesses. No Admiralty Warrant is issued unless the yacht is registered.

It has been laid down by various people in authority and out, that only a registered vessel can carry bonded (that is duty free) stores out of the country. Again, whether through kindness or ignorance I do not know, the customs have always given me clearence when I have wanted to ship bonded stores for a foreign passage. What they very reasonably do refuse is bonded stores for a short foreign trip, or bonded stores on a very small yacht which they feel is not likely to succeed in getting further than the adjacent country.

By far the biggest red herring in the whole registration argument concerns cruising abroad. In spite of repeated affirmation by all sorts of people, many of whom have official status and should know better, it is not necessary to have a yacht registered in order to cruise to foreign countries. I have owned an unregistered vessel and taken her to six countries scattered half across the world without a moment's trouble or interference. At one time I owned a small unregistered cruiser which frequently crossed the Channel and I was never asked to produce evidence that I owned the yacht.

A properly completed Bill of Sale is, in any case, recognized by authorities as proof of ownership. Anyone who buys a yacht through a competent broker will receive a Bill of Sale as a matter of course. Even if the sale is conducted privately, without the help of a broker, a Bill of Sale can easily be completed and ownership thus established (*see* Chapter 22).

On the other hand, registration is an advantage if the yacht is to be bought with borrowed money. It is impossible to get a mortgage on a yacht unless she is registered and the alternative here is to buy her through Hire Purchase. At the present time, a mortgage costs less than Hire Purchase. Though rates vary from company to company, the interest rate on Hire Purchase can be as much as double that of a mortgage.

The registration certificate, being equivalent to a birth certificate, is not lightly issued by the authorities and is a valuable document which should be carefully locked away. It shows the current and previous owners' names and addresses, as well as particulars of the vessel, her engines and so. It will also show if there is more than one owner.

Registration continues to apply to a yacht throughout her life, regardless of how she is altered. Even if she is burnt to the waterline and sunk, then salvaged and rebuilt, it is considered that she is the same vessel, just so long as the original keel is used.

In all the arguments as to whether or not a yacht should be registered, where there is a choice a strong argument appears in the matter of Limited Liability. Basically this lays down that in the case of a registered vessel, the cost to the owner of damages in the event of an accident cannot exceed £7,200. (This sum is arrived at by multiplying £24 by 300. Vessels over 300 tons pay £24 times their tonnage, and this little piece of information is merely included here for the three or four millionaires who run this size of yacht!)

However there is a gigantic snag. This limit is dependant on the owner proving he was not responsible for the accident. This can be extremely difficult, and with legal fees at the current size, the owner might easily spend more proving his innocence than he would paying for the damage.

The short answer to all this is in chapter 19 on insurance. The correct procedure is to take out a third party excess to either £50,000 or £100,000 as part of the yacht's insurance policy. This sort of excess costs around £3 to £5 for an average yacht, and has always seemed to me the biggest bargain in yachting.

Some people will bring forward the argument in favour of registration which runs like this: If you are abroad, and you get into trouble with some authority, then the local consular officials will not help unless the yacht is registered. This seems to me to ignore two facts. The first is that the vast majority of law-abiding citizens who manage to stay sober very seldom get into trouble abroad. And when they do transgress, it is more usually the person of the transgressor and not his vessel which interests the authorities. The second fact is that British consular officials tend to be among the most efficient and resourceful of all civil servants. My admittedly limited experience with them tends to make me think that they would sort out the trouble first, and make inquiries about registration afterwards.

Just to show why it is so tedious to get registration, let us follow the procedure, and see incidentally why brokers sometimes charge 15 guineas or more to cover the clerical work:

1. Apply to the local Registrar of Shipping, who is now under the Board of Trade, for registry of the yacht. This application should be a letter signed by the owner.
2. Apply to the Registrar General of the Board of Trade, General Register and Record Office of Shipping and Seamen, Llantrisant Road, Llandaff, Cardiff, Wales, for approval of the name chosen. (*See* the chapter on the subject of Names.)
3. Get the Engine Maker's Certificate (form: Surveys 118), completed by either the builder or the engine supplier.
4. Fill in an Application for Survey or Inspection (form: Surveys 6) and post together with the Engine

Registration

Maker's Certificate to the Superintendent, Mercantile Marine Office in the port in which you wish the vessel registered. (This need not be your Home Port and, indeed, only big ship ports, such as London, Glasgow, Liverpool, Leith, Greenock, Southampton etc. deal with registrations.) The Certificates listed are all obtainable from the Board of Trade or H.M. Custom Office, at the time of writing.

5. When posting off the Application for Survey and Engine Maker's Certificate, it is necessary to enclose a cheque covering the survey fee. This cheque must be made out to The Superintendent of the Mercantile Marine Office, and *not* to the Surveyors. The fee depends on the tonnage, and the tonnage is not known until the survey is complete! This typical bit of baffling bureaucracy is one reason why registration is such a nuisance.

In practice, an experienced Naval Architect can assess the likely tonnage. This enables a payment to be made and if it turns out to be insufficient, then the authorities will not be slow to render a further account.

A list of fees and expenses payable in connection with Board of Trade surveys can be seen at a Mercantile Marine Office, or bought through a bookseller.

6. The survey is carried out by a Board of Trade party. This cannot be done, in the case of a new vessel, until construction is well advanced and all deckhouses etc., are virtually complete. However, it is well worth while getting the surveyors aboard before finally painting and fitting upholstery.

The survey involves the measuring up of the internal capacity of the yacht and various deductions are made to obtain the nett registered tonnage. Basically, the gross tonnage is the total internal capacity of the yacht in cubic feet divided by one hundred. The registered tonnage is the gross tonnage less the capacity of those spaces which might be considered working areas, e.g. the 'chart-room' space which, on a small yacht, will just be the region around the chart-table. It is, of course, the *registered* tonnage which is of most interest to owners, since harbour dues and similar expenses are paid in proportion to the listed *registered* tonnage.

In order to keep registered tonnage down, an owner can designate certain areas as bosun's store or chart spaces, provided there is sufficient evidence that these areas are, in fact, what the owner says they are. Some owners contrive to get virtually the whole of the fo'c'sle made into a bosun's store and this area is then deductable.

7. The Surveyor notifies the builder (or shipyard manager in the case of an old vessel being registered for the first time) of the words to be carved therein. On the main beam will be carved the vessel's official number and her nett registered tonnage. On a beam in the bosun's store will be the words 'Bosun's store' followed by the tonnage capacity of that space, and likewise in the chart room and other deductable areas.

In the case of an old vessel, the Surveyor makes an inspection but not a full *condition* survey. This means that an unsound vessel could, in fact, be registered. However, a dilapidated hulk would not be accepted for registration. This, again, is the cause of popular misunderstanding, since some potential buyers feel that if a yacht is registered, she must be at least moderately sound.

Once the beams have been carved, the Marine Surveyor inspects them. The yard has to remember to notify him that they have completed the work.

8. The Builders' Certificate can now be completed by the Yard. This used to be a printed form but is now made up by the builder and the following form is accepted:

BUILDERS' CERTIFICATE

WE,.. certify that we built
in our building-yard at...
in the year.................................... the...............
(type of craft)............................ named..................
.... of ....
for (owner's name)...
of (address)...
the said vessel being of the following description and
dimensions:
Type of vessel...
Builders' Yard Number..
Registered Length...
Registered Breadth ....
Registered Depth...
Tonnage under Deck ....
Gross Tonnage ....
Net Tonnage..
Number of Masts...
Number of Funnels..
Number of Propellers..
Stem ....
Stern ....
Type of Engines...
Horse Power of Engines..
and that the above named and designated were the first
purchasers thereof.
IN WITNESS whereof we have hereunto affixed our
Common Seal this...................day of.....................
One thousand nine hundred and..............................

Director
Director
Secretary

9. This must be posted to the Registrar of British
   Ships at the Port of registry.
10. Together with the Builder's Certificate must be sent
    the Declaration of Ownership. This can be either
    'Declaration by Individual Owner or Transferee'
    (Form No. 2, No. 66 (Sale)) or, where there is

more than one owner, it should be 'Declaration by Joint Owners or Transferees attending together' (Form No. 5, No. 69 (Sale)).

The registration fee of £12, plus 1s for the Certificate, must be posted with either of these forms.

11. In the event of an agent, such as the yacht's designer, doing all this tedious work, he will require authority from the owner. This takes the form of an ordinary letter, merely stating that the owner authorises his agent to act on his behalf. This letter must be posted with the Builder's Certificate, Declaration of Ownership and cheque for registration fee.

12. An additional form is required to be completed and sent with the above if you appoint a person, or persons, to manage your boat, or if you are considered to be a Managing Owner. The name of this form is 'Memorandum as to the Registration of Managing Owners, etc', and is numbered c.347. The appointment of a *firm* is entirely unacceptable; the Managing Owner must be an individual.

Registration really becomes hard work when the boat is not a new one. It is essential to show proof of ownership, as well as produce a Builder's Certificate, also the engine maker's certificate. The builder may have gone out of business, or been taken over. This could also apply to the engine maker. In order to prove ownership, a Bill of Sale, or a certified copy of it, must be produced for every transfer of ownership. If one of the past owners has died, no excuses are accepted and the trustees of the deceased owner's will must handle the matter. For a boat eight years old which has had two owners, it is usually not too difficult to secure their cooperation, but for a boat twenty years old which has had six owners, the work can be complex, costly and only worth the trouble in very special circumstances.

When every change of ownership is entered on the registration certificate, it is also entered in the files at the Port of Registry. This means that a yacht which has been stolen and recovered should find its way back to the owner without trouble. It is just conceivable that a man who has no more than a Bill of Sale in his possession may have some trouble in proving he is the owner of a recovered stolen yacht. The Authorities could say that a Bill of Sale alone is not adequate proof, since it is not a document which has been lodged with any Authority. Nor is the signing of the Bill of Sale witnessed by anybody in authority. However, this contingency so very rarely arises and the owner would only be in trouble if a second person turned up to claim the yacht for himself.

In spite of all the officialdom, it is entirely possible to buy a registered yacht which does not conform to the particulars on the registration certificate. The engine may have been changed, perhaps to a different model or even a different make. In exceptional cases an owner may have taken out one engine and fitted two without remembering to inform the Registrar. When modernising a yacht, it is not unusual to fit a bigger wheelhouse or dog-house, possibly lengthen the cockpit, and even in extreme cases the yacht may be shortened or lengthened, though these are rather rare occurrences.

Any such major change affects the registration certificate and the cost of the change should be borne by the person who owns the yacht when the change is made. This means that when a boat is being bought which is registered, the buyer should carefully check the certificate against the actual yacht to avoid incurring expenses which are not properly his.

It may have occurred to the quick-thinking that it is not possible to carve the tonnage on the beam of a steel yacht. This dilemma is neatly circumvented by either writing the tonnage or other information on the beams by welding, or by punching out the appropriate words, using a centre punch.

On fibreglass yachts there are comparable techniques, such as carving the information on a piece of wood and glassing this on to a suitable bulkhead or beam.

Appendix

On the next three pages are graphs prepared by the Ship and Boatbuilders National Federation and reproduced with their permission.

They show the normal proportions for small craft of all types. If a boat departs far from these recommendations she is almost certainly a rather special boat, and probably only suitable for use in sheltered waters. Even in well-protected sailing areas a boat of unusual shape can be highly dangerous. For instance lack of beam virtually always means a poor standard of stability.

GENERAL PURPOSE DINGHIES
(including Yacht Tenders)

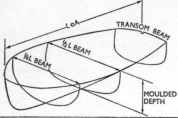

Maximum rise of floor at ½ length to be 5°
Maximum rise of floor at ¼ length to be 15°
Maximum rise of floor at transom to be 10°
(excluding boats with tucks)
Sheer at stem to be 25% higher than moulded depth
Sheer at transom to be 12½% higher than moulded depth
Fore and aft rocker to be 4% of length

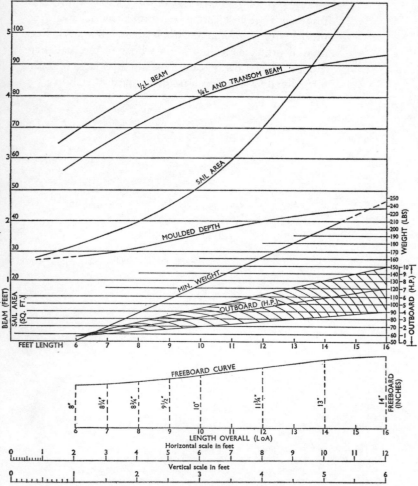

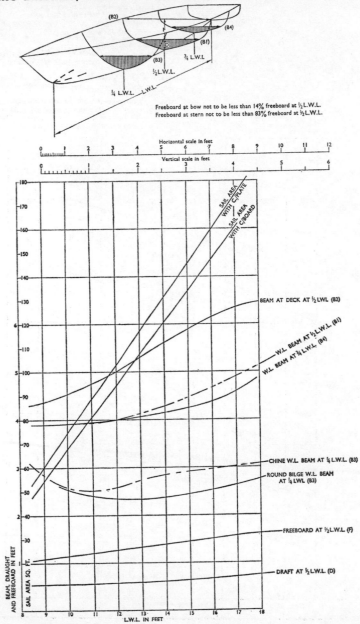

SAILING DINGHIES, INCLUDING SEMI-RACING CENTRE BOARD TYPES

Freeboard at bow not to be less than 14% freeboard at ½ L.W.L.
Freeboard at stern not to be less than 83% freeboard at ½ L.W.L.

Horizontal scale in feet

Vertical scale in feet

SAIL AREA WITH C/PLATE

SAIL AREA WITH C/BOARD

BEAM AT DECK AT ½ LWL (B2)

W.L BEAM AT ½ L.W.L. (B1)

W.L BEAM AT ¾ L.W.L. (B4)

CHINE W.L. BEAM AT ¼ L.W.L. (B3)

ROUND BILGE W.L. BEAM AT ¼ LWL (B3)

FREEBOARD AT ½ L.W.L. (F)

DRAFT AT ½ L.W.L. (D)

BEAM, DRAUGHT AND FREEBOARD IN FEET

SAIL AREA SQ. FT.

L.W.L. IN FEET

INBOARD POWERED CRAFT (SLOW AND MEDIUM SPEED)

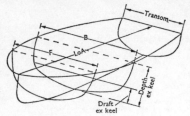

LoA = Length from stemhead to transom
B = Width at ½ L from outside of plank
D = Moulded depth at ½ L from sheer to bottom of plank (excluding keel)
F = Width ¼ L from stemhead
Transom equal to "F"
Recommended deadrise Maximum 15° (round bilge)
Maximum 13° (hard chine)

Approximate HP's shown are upper and lower limits of power range for guidance only in slow to medium speed range.

DEFINITION:
Slow : refers to craft with a speed/length ratio up to 1·5
Medium: refers to craft with a speed/length ratio in excess of 1·5 (speed/length ratio is $\frac{V}{\sqrt{L}}$ where V is the speed in knots and L is the water line length)

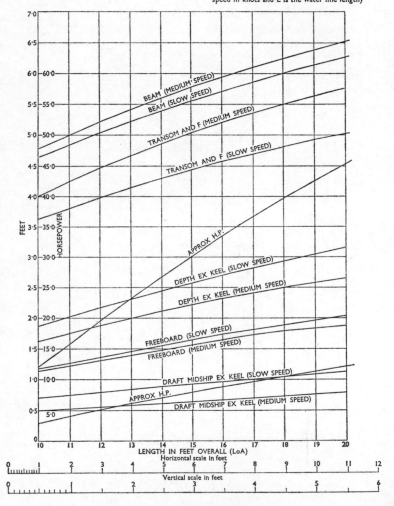